Practical LPIC-1
Linux Certification
Study Guide

David Clinton

Apress®

Practical LPIC-1 Linux Certification Study Guide

David Clinton
Toronto, Canada

ISBN-13 (pbk): 978-1-4842-2357-4   ISBN-13 (electronic): 978-1-4842-2358-1
DOI 10.1007/978-1-4842-2358-1

Library of Congress Control Number: 2016959279

Managing Director: Welmoed Spahr
Acquisitions Editor: Louise Corrigan
Development Editor: James Markham
Editorial Board: Steve Anglin, Pramila Balen, Laura Berendson, Aaron Black, Louise Corrigan, Jonathan Gennick, Todd Green, Celestin Suresh John, Nikhil Karkal, Robert Hutchinson, James Markham, Matthew Moodie, Natalie Pao, Gwenan Spearing
Coordinating Editor: Nancy Chen
Copy Editor: Mary Bearden
Compositor: SPi Global
Indexer: SPi Global
Artist: SPi Global, Image courtesy of Freepik.

Distributed to the book trade worldwide by Springer Science+Business Media New York, 233 Spring Street, 6th Floor, New York, NY 10013. Phone 1-800-SPRINGER, fax (201) 348-4505, e-mail orders-ny@springer-sbm.com, or visit www.springer.com. Apress Media, LLC is a California LLC and the sole member (owner) is Springer Science + Business Media Finance Inc (SSBM Finance Inc). SSBM Finance Inc is a Delaware corporation.

For information on translations, please e-mail rights@apress.com, or visit www.apress.com.

Apress and friends of ED books may be purchased in bulk for academic, corporate, or promotional use. eBook versions and licenses are also available for most titles. For more information, reference our Special Bulk Sales–eBook Licensing web page at www.apress.com/bulk-sales.

Any source code or other supplementary materials referenced by the author in this text is available to readers at www.apress.com. For detailed information about how to locate your book's source code, go to www.apress.com/source-code/.

Printed on acid-free paper

Contents at a Glance

About the Author xi

Introduction xiii

■Chapter 1: Topic 101: System Architecture 1

■Chapter 2: Topic 102: Linux Installation and
Package Management 17

■Chapter 3: Topic 103: Gnu and Unix Commands 31

■Chapter 4: Topic 104: Devices, Linux Filesystems, and
the Filesystem Hierarchy Standard 53

■Chapter 5: Topic 105: Shells, Scripting, and Databases 73

■Chapter 6: Topic 106: User Interfaces and Desktops................... 87

■Chapter 7: Topic 107: Administrative Tasks 99

■Chapter 8: Topic 108: Essential System Services....................... 111

■Chapter 9: Topic 109: Networking Fundamentals....................... 125

■Chapter 10: Topic 110: Security 141

■Appendix: LPIC-1 Exam Objectives... 159

Index.. 183

Contents at a Glance

Contents

About the Author xi

Introduction xiii

■Chapter 1: Topic 101: System Architecture 1

Device Management: The Linux Boot Process..................................... 1

Troubleshooting.. 5

Run Levels.. 7

Pseudo Filesystems... 10

Device Management... 11

Now Try This 13

Test Yourself 13

Answer Key 15

■Chapter 2: Topic 102: Linux Installation and
Package Management 17

Disk Partitioning 17

Install and Configure a Boot Manager 21

Shared Libraries 21

Package Managers... 23

    Local: dpkg 23

    Repositories: APT 24

    Local: RPM 27

    Repositories: yum.. 27

Now Try This 28

Test Yourself 28

Answer Key 30

■**Chapter 3: Topic 103: Gnu and Unix Commands** **31**

The Bash Shell 31

Processing Text Streams 33

File Management 37

    File Archives 40

Streams, Pipes, and Redirects 41

Managing Processes 42

    Monitoring Processes 42

    Managing Background Processes 43

    Killing Processes 45

Execution Priorities 45

Using Regular Expressions (REGEX) 46

Using vi 48

Now Try This 49

Test Yourself 49

Answer Key 52

■**Chapter 4: Topic 104: Devices, Linux Filesystems, and the
Filesystem Hierarchy Standard** **53**

Create Partitions and Filesystems 53

Maintain the Integrity of Filesystems 56

    Monitoring 56

    Preventive Maintenance 57

    Repair 57

Control Mounting and Unmounting of Filesystems 59

Manage Disk Quotas 61

Manage File Permissions and Ownership 62

    Letters 62

    Numbers (octal) 64

    Umask 64

    Using suid, sgid, and the Sticky Bit 65

Create and Change Hard and Symbolic Links 66

Find System Files and Place Files in the Correct Location 68

    Filesystem Hierarchy Standard 68

    Search Tools 69

Now Try This 70

Test Yourself 70

Answer Key 72

■Chapter 5: Topic 105: Shells, Scripting, and Databases 73

Customize and Use the Shell Environment 73

Customize and Write Simple Scripts 75

    User Inputs 76

    Testing Values 77

    Loops 78

SQL Data Management 80

Now Try This 84

Test Yourself 85

Answer Key 86

■Chapter 6: Topic 106: User Interfaces and Desktops 87

Install and Configure X11 87

Set Up a Display Manager 90

Accessibility 94

Now Try This 96

Test Yourself 96

Answer Key 97

■Chapter 7: Topic 107: Administrative Tasks 99

Manage User and Group Accounts 99

    Users 99

    Groups 102

Automate System Administration Tasks 103

    Using cron 103

    Using anacron 104

    Using at 105

Localization and Internationalization 106

Now Try This 109

Test Yourself 109

Answer Key 110

■Chapter 8: Topic 108: Essential System Services 111

Maintain System Time 111

    The Hardware Clock 111

    Network Time Protocol (NTP) 112

System Logging 114

    Using syslogd 114

    Using journald 116

    Using logger 116

    Using logrotate 117

Mail Transfer Agent Basics 118

Manage Printers and Printing 120

Now Try This 122

Test Yourself 122

Answer Key 123

■Chapter 9: Topic 109: Networking Fundamentals 125

Fundamentals of Internet Protocols 125

Transmission Protocols 125

Network Addressing 125

IPv4 126

Network Address Translation (NAT) 127

IPv6 128

Service Ports 129

Basic Network Configuration 131

Basic Network Troubleshooting 133

Configure Client Side DNS 136

Now Try This 138

Test Yourself 138

Answer Key 140

■Chapter 10: Topic 110: Security 141

System Security 141

Host Security 146

Encryption: Securing Data in Transit 148

OpenSSH 149

Passwordless Access 150

Using ssh-agent 151

X11 Tunnels 152

GnuPG Config 152

Now Try This 155

Test Yourself 155

Answer Key 157

■Appendix: LPIC-1 Exam Objectives.. 159

LPIC-1 Exam 101 159

    Topic 101: System Architecture 159

    Topic 102: Linux Installation and Package Management.................................... 161

    Topic 103: GNU and Unix Commands... 163

    Topic 104: Devices, Linux Filesystems, Filesystem Hierarchy Standard.............. 167

LPIC-1 Exam 102 170

    Topic 105: Shells, Scripting and Data Management 170

    Topic 106: User Interfaces and Desktops 172

    Topic 107: Administrative Tasks.. 173

    Topic 108: Essential System Services 175

    Topic 109: Networking Fundamentals 177

    Topic 110: Security 179

Index... 183

About the Author

David Clinton is an experienced teacher, writer, and Linux system administrator. Besides this book, he is also the author of *a book on the LPIC-3 304 certification (Linux Virtualization and High Availability)* and of a number of Linux-based video courses available at Pluralsight (`http://app.pluralsight.com/author/david-clinton`).

Introduction

First of all, welcome.

Whether you're reading this book because you've decided to earn the Linux Professional Institute's Server Professional Certification or because you simply want to learn more about Linux administration, you've made a great choice. Right now, for a thousand reasons, Linux administration skills are opening doors to some of the hottest job markets on earth. And with the ongoing explosive growth of the cloud computing world—the vast majority of it being built with Linux—the opportunities will only get richer.

Now, about this book. I chose to have the chapters closely follow the LPIC exam topics. Not only will this make it much easier for you to study for each of the two exams required for the LPIC-1 certification, but I believe that the exam objectives are actually nicely aligned with the tools you'll need in the real world. Whether or not you end up taking the exam, if you manage to learn this material, you'll have done yourself a real favor.

By far the most important element of your success, however, will have very little to do with this or any other book. No matter how much time you spend studying a book, very little of the information you read will magically translate into knowledge and skills, unless you put it to work.

If you want to really "get" this stuff, you'll have to roll up your sleeves, open up a terminal, and *do it*. As soon as you finish a chapter or a section, try out what you've learned on a real living, breathing Linux system. Even better, take on your own projects. Be ambitious. Be adventurous. Take (managed) risks.

To this end, I include suggestions for practical exercises at the end of each chapter (right before the Test Yourself quizzes). Be prepared to spend longer than you expected on some of those tasks, sometimes longer than it took you to read the chapters they're based on. Also, accept that you will probably make some mistakes that will require even more time to fix. This is all as it should be. Remember: you learn more from experience than anything else.

You will notice that I used the words "complete" and "quick" to describe this book. Let me explain what I meant. The book is complete in the sense that every concept, principle, process, and resource that might make an appearance on the exam is fully represented (even a few that are now quite obsolete and/or useless: I'm looking at you, X Font server).

However, your journey through this book may also be relatively quick, since I've tried to be as selective as possible about what I included. As you will see soon enough, I didn't even try to include every single option for every single utility, which would have been highly impractical. But it would also have been largely useless, because I don't believe any normal human being could possibly absorb page after page after page of that kind of dry, abstract information.

If you want to see the full, formal documentation for a particular Linux utility, simply consult the man pages that came preinstalled with your Linux distribution. As an example, from the command line, you can type:

```
man cp
```

Besides including only the more common command options, I also tried to avoid discussing more general IT issues that don't relate directly to the LPIC exam. It's not that they're not important, but I figured that they may only interest a relatively small number of my readers and, importantly, they're all easily accessible on the Internet. I'd like to introduce you to one of my best friends: the Internet search engine.

So if you're curious about something that isn't discussed in these pages or if a project you're working on needs greater detail, then by all means, dive in deep. But because I know that the Internet has answers to just about any question you're likely to have, I'm able to focus this book more narrowly on the curriculum that interests everyone.

Having said that, please visit our web site, bootstrap-it.com. We'll try to make your visit worthwhile and, more importantly, provide you all with the opportunity to talk to us—and to each other. Let us know how you're doing and what you think.

About Linux

There's so much I could say about Linux:

- It's the operating system used by more than 95% of the world's supercomputers.

- Google, Netflix, and Facebook? Linux, Linux, and Linux.

- The vast majority of virtual machines fired up on the leading cloud computing platforms (like Amazon's AWS) are running Linux, and that includes Microsoft's Azure!

- There's a very good chance that the software powering your car, television, smartphone, air traffic control system, and even neighborhood traffic lights is one flavor or another of Linux.

If there's innovation in the worlds of science, finance, communications, entertainment, and connectivity, it's almost certainly being driven by Linux. And if there are dozens of attractive, virus-free, secure, and reliable desktop and mobile operating systems freely available to fill all kinds of roles, those too are driven by Linux.

▓ **Note** By they way, you may be interested to know that this book was produced in its entirety on Linux, using only open source software. The whole thing: research, testing, and image processing.

The Linux Foundation recently (September 2015) estimated that, over just the past few years, collaborative projects under their umbrella have produced an estimated $5 billion in economic value. This was, again according to the Foundation, "work that would take 1,356 developers more than 30 years to replicate."

But where did all this innovation, productivity, and value come from? Who actually makes it all happen? It seems that the little operating system built a couple of decades ago by Linus Torvalds and then donated to the world, is maintained by an army of thousands of developers. According to the Linux Foundation, through 2015, 7.71 changes were accepted into the Linux kernel each HOUR and those contributions were the work of, besides Torvalds himself, more than 4,000 developers scattered around the world, many of whom, it must be noted, are sponsored by the companies they work for.

That's the *power* of open source. "Open source?" I hear you ask. "But who will support us when things go wrong?"

That's the *beauty* of open source. Because when I can't figure out how to do something or when I discover a bug in some open source software, I can usually quickly find the answer through an Internet search or, if not, there are knowledgeable and helpful folks online just waiting to help me. Try it out. You might, as I have from time to time, quickly find yourself in direct contact with the project developers themselves.

Some years ago, I wrote a white paper arguing the business case for transitioning small and medium-sized businesses from proprietary office productivity software suites (Microsoft Office) to open source alternatives (LibreOffice). When I compared the response/resolution times delivered by Microsoft with the average times seen on volunteer-staffed online OpenOffice and LibreOffice help forums, the latter would consistently produce a quicker turnaround.

Now it's your turn. All that innovation is going to need administrators to apply it to the real world. After all, we system administrators know just how little developers would get done without us. As the IT world grows and changes, you will be on the cutting edge.

Or will you? Let me tell you a story about an old friend of mine who, 25 years ago, had a great job as a Unix admin. As he tells it, the problem was that Unix (which, for the purpose of this discussion, is effectively synonymous with Linux) was getting so good at automating processes and system audits that all kinds of midlevel admins simply became unnecessary. My friend lost his job.

Could this happen to you? Absolutely. Unless, that is, you make an effort to keep up with technology as it evolves. There will be new areas to keep your eyes on (embedded tech, container virtualization, and others not yet imagined). It's the 21st century: you're never finished learning.

Nevertheless, I predict that 95% of the basic Linux skills you will learn here will probably still be in use ten and even 20 years from now. This is solid, foundational material.

About the LPIC-1 Exams

The two exams you'll need to pass to earn your Server Professional Certification (LPIC-1 101 and 102) are also known as CompTIA Linux+ LX0-103 and LX0-104. Until a few years ago, CompTIA offered a Linux certification that was so similar to the LPIC that the two eventually merged. All you have to know is that, whatever they're called, they work the same way and will get you to the same place.

That is not true of LPI's Linux Essentials (LPI-010) exam, which is a single, introductory exam that's meant for individuals with far less experience and knowledge than a candidate for the Server Professional would have. Besides those, the LPI offers two other sets of exams designed to demonstrate added skills and experience beyond those of the LPIC-1: the LPIC-2 (Linux Network Professional Certification) and LPIC-3 (Mixed Environments, Security, or Virtualization and High Availability).

This book is based on the April 2015 edition of the exams (Version 4.0). The people who maintain the certification and exams are, by design, very conservative in the way they adopt major changes, so you can be confident that the key exam topics won't be changing dramatically any time soon. Still, you should make sure that the training material on which you're relying does match the current version of the exam.

The Linux Professional Institute is vendor neutral, meaning that no one mainstream Linux distribution or software stack is favored over any other. You will therefore need to become familiar with a range of technologies. So, for example, expect to see both the Systemd and Upstart process managers, or both the apt and yum package managers. And that's a really good thing, because all of those systems are widely used (for now, at least) and all have unique valuable features. You can only gain from understanding how they all work. Success with the LPIC-1 will also automatically earn you the SUSE CLA certification.

Each exam is made up of 60 multiple choice and fill in the blank questions which must be completed within 90 minutes. To pass an exam, you will need to score 500 marks out of a total of 800. Since the questions are weighted by topic, there is no guarantee that one question will be worth the same number of marks as another. You can book an exam through the web site of either the Pearson VUE or Prometric test administration companies.

As with most technical certification exams, you will need to present the exam provider with two forms of identification, one of them a government-issued photo ID. You will also be expected to surrender any electronic devices or notebooks. (If you're very nice to the proctors, they might give them back to you once you're done.)

More than most certifications, the LPI has done a great job communicating exactly what you will need to know. You should spend some time carefully reading through the two exam objectives pages from their web site (lpi.org/study-resources/lpic-1-101-exam-objectives and lpi.org/study-resources/lpic-1-102-exam-objectives) before you begin this study and then go through them again at the end of the process to make sure you haven't missed anything. For your convenience, I've included the objectives in an appendix at the end of this book.

You will notice that each topic is given a weight between one and five. Those indicate the relative importance of a topic in terms of how large a role it will play in the exam. Table 1 is a simple chart that adds up the weights by topic to illustrate the importance of each.

Table 1. *Topics and Their Weighting*

Topic	Weight	
101	8	System Architecture
102	11	Linux Installation and Package Management
103	26	GNU and Unix Commands
104	15	Devices, Filesystems, Filesystem Hierarchy Standard
Total:	**60**	
105	10	Shells, Scripting and Data Management
106	4	User Interfaces and Desktops
107	12	Administrative Tasks
108	11	Essential System Services
109	14	Networking Fundamentals
110	9	Security
Total:	**60**	

Exam Tips

Try to arrive at the exam center as relaxed and well rested as possible. Carefully and slowly read each question and each possible response. Look for important details and for details that are only there to distract you. If you're not absolutely sure which answer is correct, try to narrow down the field a bit by eliminating answers that are obviously incorrect. You can always skip hard questions and return to them later when you've completed the rest.

Finally, remember that more people fail this exam on their first try than pass: it's designed to inspire your best effort. So don't give up.

Linux Survival Skills

Why only a single section—isn't this whole book about Linux survival skills? Well yes, but how are you going to survive between now and the time you finish reading it? Just to get you started, it might be useful to pick up a few super-critical, can't-live-without-me tools.

First, nearly everything in Linux administration will happen through the terminal. But I know that at least some of you are sitting in front of a shiny new Linux GUI interface right now and wondering where the #$%@! the terminal is (if you'll excuse my language). The answer is: that depends. Ubuntu, for instance, changes their menu design with just about every distribution, so exactly where terminal will appear on your desktop is hard to predict. In some ways, things just got more complicated with some more recent desktop manager versions, which got rid of menus altogether.

If you're not interested in poking around looking for it, you can try hitting the Alt+f2 combination and then typing terminal (or gnome-terminal) into the dialog box. Or, on some systems, Ctrl+Alt+t will get you there directly.

Once you're in the terminal, try running a command. Type:

```
pwd
```

which stands for present work directory. This is the folder (something that's almost always called a directory in Linuxland, by the way) you're currently in. You can list the files and subdirectories in your current directory with ls:

```
ls -l
```

Adding the -l argument gives you a longer, more detailed list displaying file attributes. If it's already installed (and it usually will be), you can use the nano text editor to, in this case, create and edit a new text file:

```
nano myfile.txt
```

Go ahead and type a few words and then hit Ctrl+x to save and exit. You can now quickly view your literary creation using cat:

```
cat myfile.txt
```

Try that again, but this time, type only cat my without the rest of the file name. Instead, hit the Tab key and Linux Command Completion should figure out what you're after and finish the command for you. Just hit Enter to accept the suggestion. Trust me: this one can save you a great many keystrokes and a whole lot of time over the coming years.

Let's create a new directory:

```
mkdir newplace
```

and change directory into newplace and then run pwd once again:

```
cd newplace
pwd
```

Perhaps you'd like to copy the file you just created into this directory. To do this, you'll need to keep in mind where the personal "home" directory exists in the larger Linux filesystem. Let's assume that the account is called bootstrap-it, which is therefore the name of the home directory:

```
cp /home/bootstrap-it/myfile.txt .
```

The /home/bootstrap-it/myfile.txt section identifies the file you want to copy, and the dot (.) tells the cp command to copy it to the current directory. Run ls to confirm that a copy has arrived:

```
ls
```

You can change a file's name or move it using mv:

```
mv myfile.txt mynewfile.txt
ls
```

And you can permanently delete the file using rm:

```
rm mynewfile.txt
```

To help you experiment with Linux skills without having to worry about making a mess of your important stuff, you might try working with disposable systems. One way to do that is by loading a Linux image on to a USB stick, and then booting your computer to a live Linux session. Unless you mount and play around with your existing hard drive, nothing you do will have any permanent impact on your "real" data or system settings, and nothing you do to the live filesystem will survive a reboot. This has the added potential advantage of exposing you to a wide range of Linux distributions beyond the one that you've chosen for your main work.

Of course, installing the VirtualBox package on your system will let you load virtual operating systems of nearly any flavor within your desktop environment to get a good taste of how things work in other Linux distributions.

LXC Containers

You can also create virtual machines within a working installation using LXC. An LXC container (as its called) is a fully functioning, persistent virtual "machine" that likes to imagine that it lives all by itself on your hardware (see Figure 1). You can play around in this sandbox-like environment to your heart's content and, when you break something (as you probably will), you can just destroy it and start again with a new one. I highly recommend using LXCs for exploration and experimentation. I use them myself all the time and they've saved me untold hours of heartache.

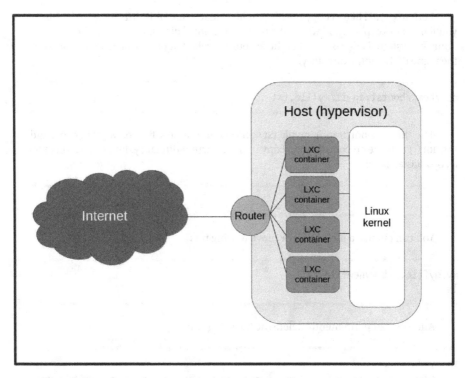

Figure 1. *LXC container architectural design*

Here are the simple steps you'll need to get started with LXC (none of this is included among the LPIC-1 exam expectations). This assumes that you're using an Ubuntu machine; some commands may be a bit different for other distributions. First, make sure that openssh is installed on your host machine (I'll talk a lot more about what that is later in the book):

```
sudo apt-get update
sudo apt-get install openssh-server
```

Now install lxc:

```
sudo apt-get install lxc
```

Then create a new container called newcon using the ubuntu template:

```
sudo lxc-create -t ubuntu -n newcon
```

Once that's done (and it should only take a minute or two), boot the new container:

```
sudo lxc-start -d -n newcon
```

The -d tells lxc to detach from the container, to allow it to survive your exit from the shell. Now let's list all the existing containers (it might take a short while before newcon is listed as fully up):

```
sudo lxc-ls --fancy
```

Assuming that the IP address for newcon (listed by our previous command) is 10.0.3.120, let's ssh into the container:

```
ssh ubuntu@10.0.3.120
```

And voila! A brand new computer playground, waiting for us to come and play! Now you've got no excuses: get to work.

■ ■ ■

## CHAPTER 1

Topic 101: System Architecture

Device Management: The Linux Boot Process

Unless you end up working exclusively with virtual machines or on a cloud platform like Amazon Web Service, you'll need to know how to do techie things like putting together real machines and swapping out failed drives. However, since those skills aren't part of the Linux Professional Institute Certification (LPIC) exam curriculum, I won't focus on them in this book. Instead, I'll begin with booting a working computer.

Whether you're reading this book because you want to learn more about Linux or because you want to pass the LPIC-1 exam, you will need to know what happens when a machine is powered on and how the operating system wakes itself up and readies itself for a day of work. Depending on your particular hardware and the way it's configured, the firmware that gets things going will be either some flavor of BIOS (Basic Input/Output System) or UEFI (Intel's Unified Extended Firmware Interface).

As illustrated in Figure 1-1, the firmware will take an inventory of the hardware environment in which it finds itself and search for a drive that has a Master Boot Record (MBR) living within the first 512 (or, in some cases, 4096) bytes. The MBR should contain partition and filesystem information, telling BIOS that this is a boot drive and where it can find a mountable filesystem.

© David Clinton 2016
D. Clinton, *Practical LPIC-1 Linux Certification Study Guide*,
DOI 10.1007/978-1-4842-2358-1_1

1

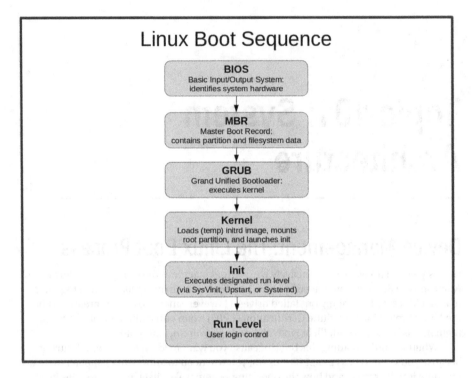

Figure 1-1. *The six key steps involved in booting a Linux operating system.*

On most modern Linux systems, the MBR is actually made up of nothing but a 512 byte file called boot.img. This file, known as GRUB Stage 1 (GRUB stands for GRand Unified Bootloader), really does nothing more than read and load into RAM (random access memory) the first sector of a larger image called core.img. Core.img, also known as GRUB Stage 1.5, will start executing the kernel and filesystem, which is normally found in the /boot/grub directory.

The images that launch from /boot/grub are known as GRUB Stage 2. In older versions, the system would use the initrd (init ramdisk) image to build a temporary filesystem on a block device created especially for it. More recently, a temporary filesystem (tmpfs) is mounted directly into memory—without the need of a block device—and an image called initramfs is extracted into it. Both methods are commonly known as initrd.

Once Stage 2 is up and running, you will have the operating system core loaded into RAM, waiting for you to take control.

■ **Note** This is how things work right now. The LPI exam will also expect you to be familiar with an older legacy version of GRUB, now known as GRUB version 1. That's GRUB **version** 1, mind you, which is not to be confused with GRUB **Stage** 1, 1.5, or 2! The GRUB we're all using today is known as GRUB version 2. You think that's confusing? Just be grateful that they don't still expect you to know about the LILO bootloader!

Besides orchestrating the boot process, GRUB will also present you with a startup menu from which you can control the software your system will load.

■ **Note** In case the menu doesn't appear for you during the start sequence, you can force it to display by pressing the right Shift key as the computer boots. This might sometimes be a bit tricky: I've seen PCs configured to boot to solid state drives that load so quickly, there almost isn't time to hit Shift before reaching the login screen. Sadly, I face no such problems on my office workstation.

As you can see from Figure 1-2, the GRUB menu allows you to choose between booting directly into the most recent Ubuntu image currently installed on the system, running a memory test, or working through some advanced options.

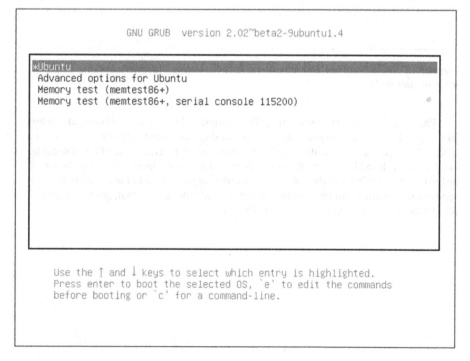

```
              GNU GRUB   version 2.02~beta2-9ubuntu1.4

 *Ubuntu
  Advanced options for Ubuntu
  Memory test (memtest86+)
  Memory test (memtest86+, serial console 115200)




      Use the ↑ and ↓ keys to select which entry is highlighted.
      Press enter to boot the selected OS, `e' to edit the commands
      before booting or `c' for a command-line.
```

Figure 1-2. A typical GRUB version 2 boot menu

3

The Advanced menu (see Figure 1-3) allows you to run in recovery mode or, if there happens to be any available, to select from older kernel images. This can be really useful if you've recently run an operating system upgrade that broke something important.

```
                 GNU GRUB   version 2.02~beta2-9ubuntu1.4

 ┌─────────────────────────────────────────────────────────────────────────┐
 │*Ubuntu, with Linux 3.13.0-24-generic                                      │
 │ Ubuntu, with Linux 3.13.0-24-generic (recovery mode)                      │
 │                                                                           │
 │                                                                           │
 │                                                                           │
 │                                                                           │
 │                                                                           │
 │                                                                           │
 │                                                                           │
 └─────────────────────────────────────────────────────────────────────────┘

     Use the ↑ and ↓ keys to select which entry is highlighted.
     Press enter to boot the selected OS, `e' to edit the commands
     before booting or `c' for a command-line. ESC to return previous
     menu.
```

Figure 1-3. *A GRUB advanced menu (accessed by selecting "Advanced options" in the main menu window)*

Pressing "e" with a particular image highlighted will let you edit its boot parameters (see Figure 1-4). I will warn you that spelling—and syntax—really, really count here. No, really. Making even a tiny mistake with these parameters can leave your PC unbootable, or even worse, bootable, but profoundly insecure. Of course, these things can always be fixed by coming back to the GRUB menu and trying again—and I won't deny the significant educational opportunities this will provide. But I'll bet that, given a choice, you'd probably prefer a quiet, peaceful existence.

```
            GNU GRUB  version 2.02~beta2-9ubuntu1.4

setparams 'Ubuntu, with Linux 3.13.0-24-generic'

                recordfail
                load_video
                gfxmode $linux_gfx_mode
                insmod gzio
                insmod part_msdos
                insmod ext2
                set root='hd0,msdos1'
                if [ x$feature_platform_search_hint = xy ]; then
                    search --no-floppy --fs-uuid --set=root --hint-bios=hd\
0,msdos1 --hint-efi=hd0,msdos1 --hint-baremetal=ahci0,msdos1   2fc9449d-1\
022-44b6-ac72-e123da5ce2b2
                else
                    search --no-floppy --fs-uuid --set=root 2fc9449d-1022-\  ↓


      Minimum Emacs-like screen editing is supported. TAB lists
      completions. Press Ctrl-x or F10 to boot, Ctrl-c or F2 for a
      command-line or ESC to discard edits and return to the GRUB
      menu.
```

Figure 1-4. *A GRUB boot parameters page (accessed by hitting "e" while an item is highlighted in the main menu window)*

Pressing "c" or Ctrl+c will open a limited command-line session.

■ **Note** You may be interested—or perhaps horrified—to know that adding rw init=/bin/bash to your boot parameters will open a full root session for anyone who happens to push the power button on your PC. If you think you might need this kind of access, I would advise you to create a secure BIOS or GRUB password to protect yourself.

Troubleshooting

Linux administrators are seldom needed when everything is chugging along happily. We normally earn our glory by standing tall when everything around us is falling apart. So you should definitely expect frantic calls complaining about black screens or strange flashing dashes instead of the cute kitten videos your user had been expecting.

If a Linux computer fails to boot, your first job is to properly diagnose the problem. And the first place you should probably look to for help is your system logs. A text record of just about everything that happens on a Linux system is saved to at least one plain text log file. The three files you should search for boot-related trouble are dmesg, kern.log, and boot.log, all of which usually live in the /var/log/ directory (some of these logs may not exist on distributions running the newer Systemd process manager).

Since, however, these logs can easily contain thousands of entries each, you may need some help zeroing in on the information you're looking for. One useful approach is to quickly scroll through say, kern.log, watching the time stamps at the beginning of each line. A longer pause between entries or a full stop might be an indication of something going wrong.

You might also want to call on some command-line tools for help. Cat will print an entire file to the screen, but often far too fast for you to read. By piping the output to grep, you can focus on only the lines that interest you. Here's an example:

```
cat /var/log/dmesg | grep memory
```

By the way, the pipe symbol (|) is typed by pressing the Shift+\ key combination. You're definitely going to need that later. (I'll discuss this kind of text manipulation a lot more in the coming chapters.)

I'm going to bet that there's something about this whole discussion that's been bothering you: if there's something preventing Linux from booting properly, how on earth are you ever going to access the log files in the first place?

Good question and I'm glad you asked. And here's my answer. As long as the hard drive is still spinning properly, you can almost always boot your computer into a live Linux session from a Linux iso file that's been written to a USB or CDRom drive, and then find and mount the drive that's giving you trouble. From there, you can navigate to the relevant log files. Here's how that might work.

You can search for all attached block devices using the command lsblk (List BLocK devices):

```
lsblk
```

Once you find your drive, create a new directory to use as a mount point:

```
sudo mkdir /tempdrive
```

Next, mount the drive to the directory you created (assuming that lsblk told you that your drive is called sdb1):

```
sudo mount /dev/sdb1 /tempdrive
```

Finally, navigate to the log directory on your drive:

```
cd /tempdrive/var/log
```

Don't worry, I'm going to talk a lot more about using each of those tools later. For now, though, I should very briefly introduce you to the way Linux manages system access.

Normal users are, by default, only allowed to edit files that they have created. System files, like those in the /var or /etc directory hierarchies, are normally accessible exclusively to the root user, or to users who have been given administrative authority. In many Linux distributions (like Ubuntu), users who need admin powers are added to the sudo group, which allows them to preface any command with the word sudo (as in sudo mkdir /tempdrive).

Invoking sudo and then entering a password temporarily gives the user full admin authority. From a security perspective, taking powers only when needed is far preferred to actually logging in as the root user.

Run Levels

There's more than one way to run a Linux computer. And, coming from the rough and tumble open source world as Linux does, there's more than one way to *control* the multiple ways you can run a Linux computer. I'll get back to that in just a minute or two.

But let's start at the beginning. One of Linux's greatest strengths is the ability for multiple users to log in and work simultaneously on a single server. This permits all kinds of savings in cost and labor and, to a large degree, is what lies behind the incredible flexibility of container virtualization.

However, there may be times when you just want to be alone. Perhaps something's gone badly wrong and you have to track it down and fix it before it gets worse. You don't need a bunch of your friends splashing around in the same pool while you work. Or maybe you suspect that your system has been compromised and there are unauthorized users lurking about. Whatever the case, you might sometimes want to temporarily change the way Linux behaves.

Linux run levels allow you to define whether your OS will be available for everyone or just a single admin user, or whether it will provide network services or graphic desktop support. Technically speaking, shutting down and rebooting your computer are also done through their own run levels.

While you will find minor differences among Linux distributions, here are the standard run levels and their designated numbers:

Boot parameter:

0: Halt

1: Single user mode

2: Multi-user, without NFS

3: Full multi-user mode

4: Unused

5: X11

6: Reboot

Run levels can be invoked from the command line using either init or telinit. Running

```
init 6
```

for instance, would cause your computer to reboot. On some distributions, you can also use commands like "shutdown" to—well—shut down. Thus:

```
sudo shutdown -h now
```

would halt ("h") a system right away and

```
sudo shutdown -h 5
```

would shut down the system, but only after 5 minutes, and

```
sudo shutdown -r now
```

would reboot.

Incidentally, since there might be other users logged into the system at the time you decide to change the run level, the shutdown command will automatically send a message to the terminals of all other logged in users, warning them of the coming change.

You can also send messages between terminals using the wall command (these messages will, of course, not reach graphical user interface [GUI] desktop users). So suppose you'd like all your colleagues to read your important memo about a new policy governing billing pizza deliveries to the company credit card. You could create a text file and cat it to the wall command:

```
cat pizza.txt | wall
```

With this, who needs Facebook?

So you've learned about the various run levels and about how they can be invoked from the command line. But how are they defined? As you've just seen, you control the way your computer will operate by setting its run level. But, as I hinted earlier, there's more than one way to do that.

Years ago, run levels were controlled by a daemon (that is, a background process) called init (also known as SysVinit). A computer's default run level was stored in a text file called inittab that lived in the /etc directory. The critical line in inittab might have looked like this:

```
id:3:initdefault
```

However, these days, if you go looking for the inittab file on your computer, the odds are that you won't find it. That's because, as computers with far greater resources became available, and as the demands of multitasking environments increased, more efficient ways of managing complex combinations of processes were needed. Back in 2006, the Upstart process manager was introduced for Ubuntu Linux and was later adopted by a number of other distributions, including Google's Chrome OS.

Under Upstart, the behavior of the computer under specific run levels is defined by files kept in directories under /etc with names like rc0.d, rc1.d, and rc2.d. The default run level in Upstart is set in the /etc/init/rc- sysinit.conf file. Its critical entry would use this syntax:

```
env DEFAULT_RUNLEVEL=3
```

Configuration files representing individual programs that are meant to load automatically under specified conditions are similarly kept in the /etc/init/ directory. Here's part of the ssh.conf file defining the startup and shutdown behavior of the Secure Shell network connectivity tool:

```
start on runlevel [2345]
stop on runlevel [!2345]
respawn
respawn limit 10 5
umask 022
```

Now that you've worked so hard to understand how both the init and Upstart systems worked, you can forget all about them. The Linux world has pretty much moved on to the systemd process manager. As of version 15.04, even Ubuntu no longer uses Upstart.

Systemd focuses more on processes than run levels. Nevertheless, you can still set your default run level by linking the default.target file in the /etc/systemd/system/ directory to the appropriate file in /usr/lib/systemd/system/.

Here's the content of default.target from a typical Fedora installation:

```
# This file is part of systemd.
#
# systemd is free software; you can redistribute it and/or modify it
# under the terms of the GNU Lesser General Public License as published by
# the Free Software Foundation; either version 2.1 of the License, or
# (at your option) any later version.
[Unit]
Description=Graphical Interface
Documentation=man:systemd.special(7)
Requires=multi-user.target
After=multi-user.target
Conflicts=rescue.target
Wants=display-manager.service
AllowIsolate=yes
```

Notice the multi-user.target values, indicating that this machine will, by default, boot to a full multi-user session. Much like the /etc/init/ directory in Upstart, /usr/lib/systemd/ contains configuration files for installed packages on systemd systems.

In fact, systemd is much more than just a simple process manager: it also includes a nice bundle of useful tools. For instance, running

```
systemctl list-units
```

will display all the currently available units and their status. A unit, by the way, is a resource that can include services, devices, and mounts. If you want to prepare, say, the Apache web server service—called httpd in Fedora—you would use systemctl and enable:

```
systemctl enable httpd.service
```

To actually start the service, you use:

```
systemctl start httpd.service
```

Pseudo Filesystems

In Linux, a filesystem is a way to organize resources—mostly files of one sort or another—in a way that makes them accessible to users or system resources. In a later chapter, I'll discuss the structure of a number of particularly common Linux filesystems (like ext3, ext4, and reiserFS) and how they can enhance security and reliability. For now, though, let's look at a specific class: the pseudo filesystem.

Since the word pseudo means fake, it's reasonable to conclude that a pseudo filesystem is made up of files that don't actually exist. Instead, the objects within such a structure simply *represent* real resources and their attributes. Pseudo filesystems are generated dynamically when your computer boots.

The /dev directory contains files representing hardware devices—both real and virtual. That's why, as you saw earlier in this chapter, a /dev address (/dev/sdb1) is used to identify and mount a hard drive. As you've also seen, lsblk displays all recognized physical block drives. Running

```
lsblk -a
```

however, will also show you *all* the block devices currently represented in /dev (even virtual devices).

The contents of the /sys directory represent the sysfs system and contain links to devices. The /sys/class/block directory, therefore, would include links to block devices, while the /sys/class/printer directory would contain links to printers.

The files within the /proc directory contain runtime system information. That is to say, a call to files within this hierarchy will return information about a system resource or process. Applying cat to the cpuinfo file, for instance,

```
cat /proc/cpuinfo
```

will return a technical description of your computer's CPU. Note however that poking the cpuinfo file with the "file" command reveals something interesting:

```
file /proc/cpuinfo cpuinfo: empty
```

It's empty!

You should spend some time exploring these directories. You might be surprised what you uncover.

You can quickly access subsets of the information held by these filesystems through a number of terminal commands: lspci will output data on all the PCI and PCI Express devices attached to your system. Adding the -xvvv argument:

```
lspci -xvvv
```

10

will display more verbose information; lsusb will give you similar information for USB devices; and lshw (list hardware) will—especially when run as the root—display information on your entire hardware profile.

Even though it doesn't contain pseudo files, I should also mention the /run directory hierarchy, since its contents are volatile, meaning that they are deleted each time you shut down or reboot your PC. So /run is therefore a great place for processes to save files that don't need to hang around indefinitely.

Device Management

Up to this point, you've seen how Linux learns enough about its hardware neighborhood to successfully boot itself, how it knows what kind of working environment to provide, and how it identifies and organizes hardware devices. Now let's find out how to manage these resources.

First, I should explain the role played by kernel modules in all this. Part of the genius of Linux is that its kernel—the software core that drives the whole thing—permits real-time manipulation of some of its functionality through modules. If you plug in a USB drive or printer, for instance, the odds are that Linux will recognize it and make it instantly available to you. This might seem obvious, but getting it right in a complicated world with thousands of devices in use is no simple thing.

Hotplug devices—like USB drives and cameras—can be safely added to a computer while it's actually running (or "hot"). Invoking udev, using communication provided by the D-Bus system, should recognize the device and automatically load a kernel module to manage it (see Figure 1-5).

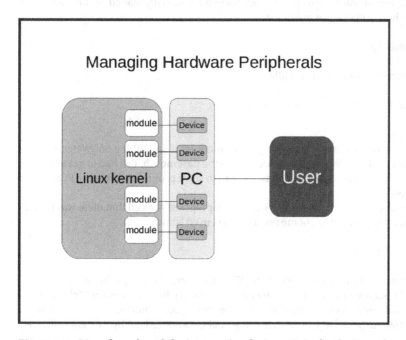

Figure 1-5. Linux kernel modules interpreting device activity for the Linux kernel

11

By and large, if you've got to open your computer's case to add a device, it's going to be of the coldplug variety: meaning, you shouldn't try to insert your device with the computer running. While I'm on that topic, it can't hurt to remind you that you should never touch exposed circuit boards without fully grounding yourself first. I've seen very expensive devices destroyed by static charges too small to be felt by humans.

Either way, once your device is happily plugged in, the appropriate kernel module should do its job connecting what needs connecting. But there will be times when you'll need to control modules yourself. To define device naming and behavior, you can edit its udev rules.d file. If there isn't already a .rules file specific to your device, you can create one in any one of these directories:

```
/etc/udev/rules.d/
/run/udev/rules.d/
/usr/lib/udev/rules.d/
```

If there are overlapping .rules files in more than one of those locations, udev will read and execute the first one it finds using the above order.

Even if a kernel module is not actually loaded into memory, it might well be installed. You can list all currently installed modules using this rather complex application of the find tool:

```
find /lib/modules/$(uname -r) -type f -iname "*.ko"
```

where *uname -r* will return the name of the kernel image that's currently running (to point "find" to the correct directory), the object type is "*file*" and the file extension is *.ko*.

Running lsmod will list only those modules that are actually loaded. To load an installed module, you can use modprobe:

```
sudo modprobe lp
```

which will load the printer driver, while:

```
sudo modprobe -r lp
```

will remove the module.

Don't think that manually managing kernel modules is something only veteran administrators and developers need to do. In just the past month, I've had to get my hands dirty with this task not once, but twice, and to solve problems on simple PCs, not rack-mounted servers!

The first time occurred when I logged into a laptop and noticed that there was no Wi-Fi. The usual troubleshooting got me nowhere, so I used lshw:

```
sudo lshw -C network
```

to see what the system had to say about the Wi-Fi interface. The phrase "network UNCLAIMED" showed up next to the entry for the adapter. Because it wasn't "claimed," the adapter had never been assigned an interface name (like wlan0) and it was, of course, unusable. I now suspect that the module was somehow knocked out by a recent software update.

The solution was simple. With some help from a quick Google search built around the name of this particular Wi-Fi model, I realized that I would have to manually add the ath9k module. I did that using:

```
sudo modprobe ath9k
```

and it's been living happily every after.

The second surprise happened when I couldn't get a browser-based web conferencing tool to recognize my webcam. Again, all the usual tricks produced nothing, but Internet searches revealed that I wasn't the first user to experience this kind of problem. Something was causing the video camera module to crash, and I needed a quick way to get it back on its feet again without having to reboot my computer. I first needed to unload the existing module:

```
sudo rmmod uvcvideo
```

Then it was simply a matter of loading it again, and we were off to the races:

```
sudo modprobe uvcvideo
```

Now Try This

Let's imagine that you recently added a PCI Express network interface card (NIC) to your system. Because it's new, udev assigned it the name em1 rather than em0 (the name used by your existing integrated NIC). The problem is that you've hard coded em0 into various scripts and programs, so they all expect to find a working interface with that name. But as you want to connect your network cable to the new interface, em0 will no longer work. Since you're far too lazy to update all your scripts, how can you edit a file in the /etc/udev/rules.d/ directory to give your new NIC the name em0?

■ **Note** I would strongly advise you to create a backup copy of any file you plan to edit, and then make sure you restore your original settings once you're done!

Test Yourself

1. Pressing Ctrl+c in the GRUB menu will:

    a. Allow you to edit a particular image

    b. Open a command line session

    c. Initiate a memory test

    d. Launch a session in recovery mode

2. Adding rw init=/bin/bash to your boot parameters in GRUB will:

    a. Allow root access on booting

    b. Launch a session in recovery mode

    c. Display the most recent contents of the /var/log/dmesg file

    d. Allow logged messages to be edited

3. sudo is:

    a. Another name for the Linux root user

    b. The command that mounts devices in the root directory

    c. The most direct tool for changing system run levels

    d. A system group whose members can access admin permissions

4. On most Linux systems, run level 1 invokes:

    a. Single user mode

    b. X11 (graphic mode)

    c. Reboot

    d. Full multi-user mode

5. On Linux systems running systemd, the default run level can be found in:

    a. /etc/systemd/system/inittab

    b. /lib/systemd/system/default.target

    c. /etc/systemd/system/default.target

    d. /etc/init/rc-sysinit.conf

6. You can find links to physical devices in:

    a. /dev

    b. /etc/dev

    c. /sys/lib

    d. /proc

7. Which is the quickest way to display details on your network device?

   a. lsblk

   b. lspci

   c. cat /proc/cpuinfo

   d. lshw

8. Which tools are used to watch for new plug-in devices?

   a. udev and modprobe

   b. rmmod and udev

   c. modprobe, uname, and D-Bus

   d. udev and D-Bus

9. The correct order udev will use to read rules files is:

   a. /etc/udev/rules.d/ /usr/lib/udev/rules.d/ /run/udev/rules.d/

   b. /usr/lib/udev/rules.d/ /run/udev/rules.d/ /etc/udev/rules.d/

   c. /etc/udev/rules.d/ /run/udev/rules.d/ /usr/lib/udev/rules.d/

   d. /etc/udev/rules.d/ /run/udev/rules.d/

10. You can load a kernel module called lp using:

   a. sudo modprobe lp

   b. sudo modprobe load lp

   c. sudo modprobe -l lp

   d. sudo rmmod lp

Answer Key

1. b, 2. a, 3. d, 4. a, 5. c, 6. a, 7. b, 8. d, 9. c, 10. a

CHAPTER 2

■ ■ ■

Topic 102: Linux Installation and Package Management

I'm not sure there's all that much tying the various expectations of LPIC-1 exam topic 102 together into any kind of cohesive whole. It is true that they all address concerns shared by Linux administrators and, broadly speaking, concerns related to prepare stable and productive compute environments. So there's that.

Either way, this chapter will discuss partitioning your storage space and controlling the boot process through a boot manager, working with the software libraries shared by individual software packages, and the critical task of acquiring and managing the fantastic collections of free software provided by various online Linux repositories.

Disk Partitioning

The way you organize the drive or drives that will host your operating system and all your data can have a significant impact on both the performance and security of your entire operation. A successful installation design will carefully balance two sometimes conflicting objectives: accessibility and separation. You want your users to have access to all the resources and tools they'll need to get their work done, but you also want to protect sensitive or private data from unnecessary exposure.

Intelligent partitioning can take you a long way toward achieving those goals. A disk partition effectively divides a single physical disk into smaller logical parts. Such divisions make it easy to isolate resources, limiting access to only those users and processes that need it.

A common default partition scheme would create three partitions: one for the root filesystem (designated with a single forward slash [/]), one for the boot directory, and the third for the system swap file. A swap file, by the way, is a section of your drive that is set aside to emulate system memory (RAM) for times when demand exceeds the limits of your actual RAM. It is a widespread practice to set your swap file to the same size as your real RAM.

© David Clinton 2016
D. Clinton, *Practical LPIC-1 Linux Certification Study Guide*,
DOI 10.1007/978-1-4842-2358-1_2

$ df Filesystem	1K-blocks	Used Available Use%	Mounted on
/dev/sdb2	472675276	123047744 325593964	28% / none
4 /sys/fs/cgroup	0	4	0%
udev	3628000	4 3627996 1%	/dev
tmpfs	727808	1896 725912 1%	/run
none	5120	0 5120 0%	/run/lock
none	3639036	50072 3588964 2%	/run/shm
none	102400	56 102344 1%	/run/user
/dev/sdb1	499008	3456 495552 1%	/boot/efi

In the above example, running df against my system shows partitions for both root and boot, but also virtual partitions for the pseudo filesystems /sys and /dev, and four others related to the nonpersistent /run directory. This is all standard stuff.

You, however, might prefer to create separate partitions for the directories under, say, /etc or /lib. In Figure 2-1 (a screenshot taken from the Ubuntu server installation process), besides having separate partitions for root (/) and /home, the /var directory hierarchy is kept on its own, perhaps to ensure that logs and other automatically generated data files aren't able to grow so large that they swallow the entire drive. Don't think that can't happen: I've seen log files grow to more than 100GB when they're not properly rotated.

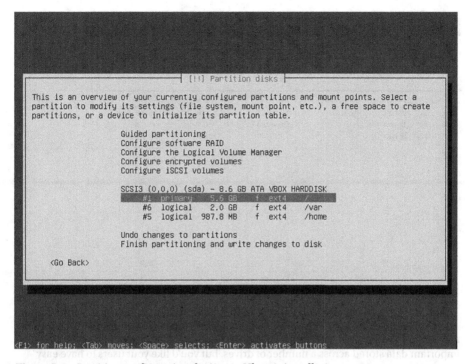

Figure 2-1. Partition configuration during an Ubuntu installation process

Disk partitioning is normally done on a new or repurposed drive as part of the installation process. Resizing and adding partitions on an existing production drive can be done, but it's risky. Even if you carefully and correctly work through all the steps, there is a chance that some or all of your data could be permanently lost. Having said that, editing partitions can be done, and if you're ready to accept the risk, I would recommend using the GUI GParted tool (see Figure 2-2) to do it.

Partition	File System	Mount Point	Size	Used	Unused	Flags
/dev/sdb1	fat32	/boot/efi	488.28 MiB	4.34 MiB	483.94 MiB	boot
/dev/sdb2	ext4	/	458.09 GiB	143.41 GiB	314.68 GiB	
/dev/sdb3	linux-swap		7.19 GiB	7.50 KiB	7.19 GiB	

Figure 2-2. *The GParted partition management tool in action*

Disk partitioning is good for making a single disk appear as multiple drives, but there may be times when you want to make multiple disks appear as one. Suppose you've got important data stored across a number of drives, but you'd like your users to have easy and intuitive access to everything as though it's all on a single disk. Or perhaps you're not sure exactly how much space you might require for a particular partition a few months down the line and need an easy way to change things later. Working with the Logical Volume Manager (LVM) is one possible solution.

■ **Note** Besides LVM, you can also use "add mount points" to your /etc/fstab file to make specified resources appear as though they are somewhere else. I'll talk more about fstab in a later chapter.

For the LPIC-1 exam, you are expected to be familiar with no more than the basic features of LVM. To that end, I will illustrate only three basic commands that can be used on a system with LVM enabled.

First, though, you should be aware that LVM uses the acronym **PV** to represent a physical volume, **VG** for volume groups (collections of one or more physical volumes), and **LV** for logical volumes.

To create a new volume group, you use the vgcreate command and specify the name you'd like to give your group and the physical partitions you want to include:

```
sudo vgcreate my-new-vg /dev/sdb2 /dev/sdb3
```

Once you have a volume group, you can use it as part of a new logical volume:

```
sudo lvcreate -n my-new-lv my-new-vg
```

Finally, you can scan for all logical volumes on your system using lvscan:

```
sudo lvscan
```

Install and Configure a Boot Manager

It may not be immediately obvious why you would ever want to create or edit GRUB on a running Linux system. After all, it's running already: what needs fixing?

Well, suppose your GRUB configuration has been corrupted by an unsuccessful attempt to install a second OS on your drive. You could easily be left with a computer that doesn't boot. You might also simply want to manually edit the choices and basic settings that are included in the GRUB menu. Either way, these are important tools.

Assuming that the drive on which you want to install GRUB is called sdb, installing the software is as simple as:

```
sudo grub-install /dev/sdb
```

or, on Fedora machines:

```
sudo grub2-install /dev/sdb
```

What will actually appear in your GRUB menu is controlled by settings kept in the /etc/default/grub file and templates in the /etc/grub.d/ directory. When you're done editing your settings, you must run either grub-mkconfig (grub2-mkconfig for Fedora) or update-grub. These will update a script: either /boot/grub/grub.cfg or /boot/grub/menu. lst, depending on your particular distribution. When those scripts are actually run the next time you start up, your new GRUB configuration will be active.

While it is important for you to be aware of all that, in the real world you might prefer to use a really handy tool called Boot-Repair. I don't normally recommend GUI tools—after all, real admins don't use mice—but this one can save you so much time and trouble that it's just too good to ignore. You can find everything you'll need to run Boot-Repair here: https://help.ubuntu.com/community/Boot-Repair

Shared Libraries

Linux libraries, which allow software packages to properly interact with their local environment, are another part of the incredible success of Linux. The fact that programmers can configure their software to load libraries with all the environment data it will need means that there's no need for them to spend time reinventing the wheel, and that they can compile much smaller packages. Developers are also freed to focus on the core functionality of their specific packages.

Linux libraries come in two flavors: static (whose contents are incorporated by a program into its own code at installation time) and dynamic (whose contents are accessed whenever a program needs information).

Let's take a look at the naming convention used by library files. As you might expect, one great place to find shared libraries would be in the /lib directory. Here's an example:

```
libip6tc.so.0.1.0
```

In this name "*lib*" tells us that this file is a library, "*ip6tc*" would be the package name, "*so*" identifies it as a dynamic library ("so" stands for shared object), and *0.1.0* is the package version. If this were a static library, there would be an "*a*" instead of the "so."

A single package can be dependent on dozens of libraries. Normally, Linux package managers take care of handling dependencies for you (as you'll see in just a few minutes). But being aware of how it works can be helpful for troubleshooting when things go wrong or for when you need to build your own libraries.

You can use ldd to display the libraries that a particular package depends on. As you can see, the VLC multimedia player requires quite a collection:

```
$ ldd /usr/bin/vlc
linux-vdso.so.1  =>  (0x00007ffc4fbc8000)
libvlc.so.5  =>  /usr/lib/libvlc.so.5 (0x00007fc5ba898000)
libpthread.so.0  =>    /lib/x86_64-linux-gnu/libpthread.so.0
(0x00007fc5ba678000)
libdl.so.2      =>    /lib/x86_64-linux-gnu/libdl.so.2 (0x00007fc5ba470000)
libc.so.6      => (0x00007fc5ba0a8000)    /lib/x86_64-linux-gnu/libc.so.6
libvlccore.so.7 (0x00007fc5b9dc0000) => /usr/lib/libvlccore.so.7
/lib64/ld-linux-x86-64.so.2 (0x00007fc5baab8000)
librt.so.1   =>  /lib/x86_64-linux-gnu/librt.so.1 (0x00007fc5b9bb8000)
libidn.so.11  =>  /usr/lib/x86_64-linux-gnu/libidn.so.11 (0x00007fc5b9980000)
libm.so.6  =>  /lib/x86_64-linux-gnu/libm.so.6 (0x00007fc5b9678000)
libdbus-1.so.3 => /lib/x86_64-linux-gnu/libdbus-1.so.3 (0x00007fc5b9430000)
```

If you want to list all the libraries stored in the current cache, use:

```
ldconfig -p
```

Since that will be a very long list (nearly 1,800 lines in my case), you might like to narrow down the search just a bit. By piping the output to grep, you can filter by a search string. This example will display only those libraries whose names include the phrase "usb":

```
ldconfig -p | grep usb
```

Like just about everything else you will see in this book, you should take a moment, open up a terminal, and try this for yourself. Don't worry, I'll still be here when you get back.

Library data are actually stored in the /etc/ld.so.cache file. The cache gets its information through links in the /etc/ld.so.conf file.

If you have created your own library, you'll need to let Linux in on the good news. You do that by creating a plain text file in the /etc/ld.so.conf.d/ directory that contains nothing but the absolute path to the new library (i.e., /home/myname/libraries). You will name the file something like: my_lib_name.conf. On some distributions at least, the contents of /etc/ld.so.cache are exported to the LD_LIBRARY_PATH variable.

In any case, to apply the new links, you'll have to run ldconfig.

Package Managers

Giving a piece of software all the tender loving care it needs to function effectively can sometimes be a challenge. A program will need enough memory to go about its business, and often some space where it can save records of what it's been doing. And as you've just learned, it also needs to know how to access local resources and will therefore rely rather heavily on the active presence of system libraries.

If you had to arrange for all that yourself, downloading and installing new software would require that you track down the appropriate package on the Internet, do the necessary research to confirm that there are no conflicts with other software or with your hardware profile, and manually install all the needed libraries. And that's besides confirming that the package itself isn't actually malware and then keeping up with security patches and upgrades through the life cycle of the product.

All that can be done, but most of us would probably do a lot less of it if it were only our choice.

Fortunately, Linux package managers were designed to reliably take care of all those details without your help. The two dominant curated repositories I'll discuss here—the APT system for Debian/Ubuntu and the YUM manager for Red Hat/CentOS/Fedora—will deliver secure, provisioned, and highly functional software with literally nothing more than a single mouse click (or, better yet, with a one-line terminal command).

Each of these two systems is actually part of a two-tier infrastructure: one tier for managing packages locally and the other as an interface with online, managed software repositories. Let's start with the Debian/Ubuntu world.

Local: dpkg

If you've already downloaded or created your own .deb package file, you can manage it locally through dpkg. The dpkg environment settings are configured through the /etc/dpkg/dpkg.cfg file. Debian package files will look something like this:

```
my_package_2.4.1-1_amd64.deb
```

The package name is my_package, 2.4.1-1 is the version number, amd64 is the architecture it's built for (i.e., 64 bit; 32 bit packages would use i386), and .deb tells us that it's built as a Debian package.

To directly install your package, use:

```
sudo dpkg -i my_package_2.4.1-1_amd64.deb
```

You can unpack the package without installing it by adding the --unpack argument:

```
sudo dpkg --unpack my_package_2.4.1-1_amd64.deb
```

You can remove, purge, and reconfigure packages using, respectively, -r, -P, and dpkg-reconfigure. Note that you only need the package name for these operations:

```
sudo dpkg -r my_package
```

```
sudo dpkg -P my_package
sudo dpkg-reconfigure my_package
```

You can list all currently installed packages (including those from the repositories) using:

```
dpkg -l
```

or, if you need simpler output as part of some larger operation:

```
dpkg --get-selections
```

Using dpkg -s will display details of the specified package:

```
dpkg -s zip
```

Repositories: APT

Most of your work with packages will be performed through the online repositories. On Debian and Ubuntu computers (among others) that, happily, means APT. The /etc/apt/ sources.list contains a list of registered repositories. The sources.list file was populated during installation, but you can edit it by hand when necessary. Here are a few lines from my sources file:

```
deb http://ca.archive.ubuntu.com/ubuntu/ trusty main restricted
deb-src http://ca.archive.ubuntu.com/ubuntu/ trusty main restricted
deb http://security.ubuntu.com/ubuntu  trusty-security universe
deb-src http://security.ubuntu.com/ubuntu trusty-security universe
deb http://security.ubuntu.com/ubuntu trusty-security multiverse
deb-src http://security.ubuntu.com/ubuntu trusty-security multiverse
```

You will notice that each line includes an Internet URL—the target address of a particular repository. The field that follows is comprised of the name of the repo's specific release, in this case, it's "trusty main" or "trusty-security". Trusty is the codename for Ubuntu 14.04. The final field contains the repository *component* (restricted, universe, etc.).

Once APT is configured to meet your needs, it's time to put it to work. You should be careful to update apt-get to make sure that your local system's record of available packages is in sync with the upstream repos:

```
sudo apt-get update
```

You're now ready to download software. If you don't know the name of the package you're after, you might like to search through the thousands of available titles using the GUI tool, Synaptic (see Figure 2-3).

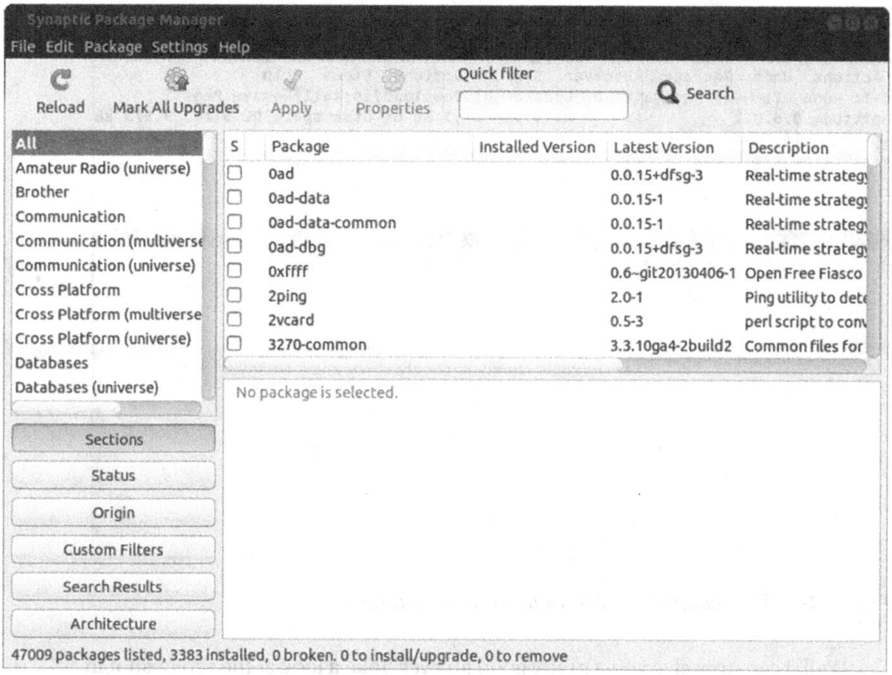

***Figure 2-3.** The Synaptic package manager. Note the "search by category" choices on the left.*

You won't need to know anything about Synaptic for the LPIC exam, but that doesn't make it any less of a handy resource. On the other hand, you *will* need to be familiar with Aptitude. You launch Aptitude from the command line:

```
sudo aptitude
```

It took me a long time to figure out what value Aptitude (see Figure 2-4) actually had. It's not a true GUI application, so if you're one of those who doesn't like using the command line (not that I would suggest even for a second that you're one of *those*), you'd be better off with Synaptic. But it's not really a command-line tool either. So who needs it?

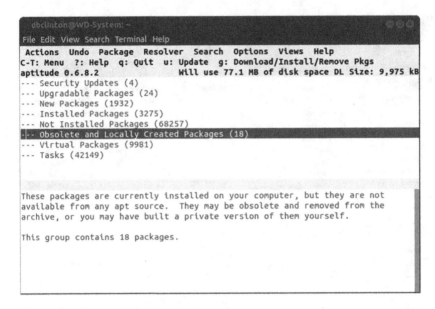

Figure 2-4. The semigraphic Aptitude package manager

Well, I can now give you a pretty good answer. Take a look at the screenshot in Figure 2-4. Notice how the menu groups packages by various categories. Now that "Obsolete and Locally Created Packages" is highlighted, I only need to click Enter and I'll be taken to a new menu that lists all 18 of them. I could then use the arrow keys to move up and down the list, and click Enter again to be shown the full profile and status of whichever package I'm after. I think you can see the value in that.

Still, let's go back to the command line and get some real work done. To install a new program, let's say VLC, you use apt-get install:

```
sudo apt-get install vlc
```

The command apt-get install -s will display package dependencies without installing. You can remove a package using apt-get remove:

```
sudo apt-get remove vlc
```

Like apt-get upgrade, apt-get dist-upgrade will install the newest versions of all installed packages. But it will also make "intelligent" decisions about package conflicts and remove any unnecessary dependencies.

Besides apt-get, the APT system also provides the apt-cache family of commands:

```
apt-cache showpkg vlc
```

This will display statistics on the specified package. The command *apt-cache depends* returns package dependencies and *apt-cache unmet* will report any unmet dependencies.

Local: RPM

The RPM package manager is used by a large number of important Linux distributions, including Red Hat Enterprise Linux, CentOS, and Fedora. Broadly speaking, it works in much the same way as APT, although from a parallel repository system. Like dpkg, rpm is meant to manage local software packages, while yum—much like APT—handles upstream, curated repositories. Let's begin with a look at an rpm file:

```
apacheds-2.0.0-M20-x86_64.rpm
```

Here, *apacheds* is the name of the package, *2.0.0-M20* is the version number, *x86_64* is the architecture, and *.rpm* indicates that the file is an rpm archive; rpm -i will install a package:

```
rpm -i apacheds-2.0.0-M20-x86_64.rpm
```

You can verify the integrity of a file by using rpm –V:

```
rpm -V apacheds-2.0.0-M20-x86_64.rpm
```

And rpm -vK will return the file's checksum:

```
rpm -vK apacheds-2.0.0-M20-x86_64.rpm
```

Using rpm -i --test (followed by the file name) will check for dependencies, rpm -U will upgrade a file to the latest version, rpm -q httpd will display the current installed version number of, in this case, the Apache web server package, and rpm -e httpd will remove the package (note that you don't need to include the full package name for those last two commands).

You can also query packages using rpm. -q –a, which will list all currently installed packages:

```
rpm -q -a
```

Using -qid and the name of a package will display detailed information about it:

```
rpm -qid bash
```

Repositories: yum

Installing and maintaining repo-based software in the RHEL family of distributions is handled by YUM. Repository preferences are configured through files in the /etc/yum.repos.d/ directory and by the /etc/yum.conf configuration file. Using yum install will, predictably, install a package:

```
sudo yum install httpd
```

Similarly, *yum remove* and *yum update* will do pretty much what their names suggest. You can search for a package using *yum search httpd* and list all available packages with yum list. Using *yum list installed* will search only through currently installed packages. You can download a package without installing it using:

```
yumdownloader --resolve httpd
```

where --resolve adds dependencies to the download.

You can use yum search to search for packages:

```
yum search libreoffice
```

Once you've found the name of a package you're interested in, you can use yum info to display more detailed information:

```
yum info libreoffice-writer.i686
```

Finally, you should be aware that .rpm files are normally compressed with the cpio archiver. If you want to access files from the archive, you will use the rpm2cpio tool. Piping a .rpm package to cpio using the -i (restore the archive) and -d (create leading directories) arguments will restore the entire archive:

```
rpm2cpio apacheds-2.0.0-M20-x86_64.rpm | cpio -id
```

Now Try This

Sometimes the packages included in your distribution's official software repositories can fall behind the latest cutting-edge versions available directly from the developers themselves, but you might sometimes need the latest version. The Calibre e-book reader is an example of a project that often adds features too quickly for some public repos to keep up.

Try adding Calibre's private repository (PPA; Personal Package Archive) to your system (either by editing the sources file directly or from the command line) and then installing it. You will probably need a bit of help from a search engine like Google.

Test Yourself

1. Which of these is NOT commonly given its own partition?

    a. SWAP

    b. /etc

    c. /

    d. /dev

2. The primary goal of LVM is to allow you to ...

   a. Separate resources into different partitions

   b. Provide common access to shared libraries

   c. Install GRUB on a boot drive

   d. Provide easy access to resources on distributed partitions

3. Changes to GRUB settings will not take effect until you run ...

   a. grub-mkconfig

   b. grub-install /dev/sdb

   c. /etc/default/grub

   d. /etc/grub.d/update.sh

4. Which of these is incorporated into program code during installation?

   a. Dynamic libraries

   b. Shared libraries

   c. Static libraries

   d. Lending libraries

5. Which of these will list all libraries currently stored in cache?

   a. ldd

   b. libip6tc.so.0.1.0

   c. ldconfig -p

   d. ldconfig

6. When you create your own library, you need to ...

   a. Add its name to the /etc/ld.so.cache file

   b. Add a file pointing to its location to the /etc/ld.so.conf.d directory

   c. Add a file pointing to its location to the /etc/ld.so.conf directory

   d. Run ldconfig -u

7. _____ manages online repo-based software for Red Hat Linux:

   a. YUM

   b. APT

   c. dpkg

   d. rpm

8. You can install VLC on a Debian system using:

    a. apt-get install vlc

    b. apt-get -i vlc

    c. yum -i vlc

    d. dpkg install vlc

9. You can delete VLC from a Debian system using:

    a. apt-get -r vlc

    b. apt-get -delete vlc

    c. dpkg -i vlc

    d. apt-get remove vlc

10. YUM repository settings are defined by:

    a. /etc/yum.conf.d/

    b. /etc/yum.repos/yum.conf

    c. /yum/repos.d/

    d. /etc/yum.repos.d/

Answer Key

1. b, 2. d, 3. a, 4. c, 5. c, 6. b, 7. a, 8. a, 9. d, 10. d

CHAPTER 3

■ ■ ■

Topic 103: Gnu and Unix Commands

If, as is often said, just about everything in Linux is a plain text file, then it stands to reason that a great deal of Linux administration should depend on intelligently handling plain text. Through the course of this book, you'll discover just how true this is and just how much can be accomplished through manipulating text streams. In this chapter, you'll work through the very rich collection of Linux text, file, and process management tools.

Let's begin with the Linux shell. Whenever you open a terminal or log in to a non-GUI environment, you are creating a new shell session. The command prompt you face is waiting for you to type in commands, but the way it will interpret those commands depends on which shell interpreter you're using. The differences between various Linux shells are subtle and you might actually go some time without even being aware of which one you're using. But it is important to know that the LPIC exam is built on the Bash shell.

One more general point before you get started here. When it comes to working with Bash, spelling counts a great deal. And so does capitalization. If a file name or command uses, say, all lowercase letters, then that's usually the only way that the command interpreter will recognize it, and changing things around will cause your command to fail.

The Bash Shell

Every shell comes with environment variables. Type:

```
echo $USER
```

for instance, and I bet you'll see your name, or at least the name of the account you used to log in. This works because your shell has a built-in variable called USER that is populated with the value of the account name.

A particularly useful value you should be aware of is PWD. Type:

```
echo $PWD
```

What did Bash print? Your current directory, right? (PWD stands for Present Work Directory.) Now move to a different directory:

© David Clinton 2016
D. Clinton, *Practical LPIC-1 Linux Certification Study Guide*,
DOI 10.1007/978-1-4842-2358-1_3

```
cd /etc
```

Then run echo $PWD again. The output has changed. You can actually access this value more quickly by simply typing:

```
pwd
```

If you'd like to see a list of all the current variables (but not local variables or functions, things I'll talk about at length in a later chapter), type:

```
env
```

The set command, by the way, will display all shell variables, *including* local variables and functions.

You can create a new variable by typing something like this:

```
myvariable=hello
```

If you want to confirm that it worked, type:

```
echo $myvariable
```

The word "hello" should appear. If you type echo myvariable without the $, the string "myvariable" will print to the screen. It's the dollar sign that tells Bash that you're referencing a variable and not just playing with text.

So now you're the happy and proud owner of a shiny new shell variable. The problem is that it will only exist for the shell you're currently using. If you want it to be available to new shells that you might launch beneath this one, you'll have to export it:

```
export myvariable
```

You can use a close cousin of *set* to destroy your variable by typing:

```
unset myvariable
```

Another resource you should know about is uname. Typing it will return the system (Linux). Typing it with -a, however:

```
uname -a
```

will display a great deal more about your kernel and installation.

Here are two or three really useful tips before I move on. You'll definitely thank me for them at some point in your careers. Open up a terminal and press the Up arrow. You should see the most recent command you used appear at the command line, ready to be used again. Press the Up arrow a few more times and you'll see all your recent commands displayed in reverse order. This labor-saving feature is brought to you courtesy of the .bash_history file.

You'll use the *less* text reader program to view the file to see what's there. First, make sure that you're in your home directory:

```
cd ~
less .bash_history
```

Feel free to use the Arrow keys to move up and down through the file, and then type q when you want to exit. As you can see, it's a list of your last 2,000 commands. You can quickly access the contents of the file using the *history* command. And, of course, you can narrow down your search with grep:

```
history | grep .bash_history
```

As I mentioned in the introduction to the book, you will also enjoy using the Tab key for command completion. Start typing a command—say the first four letters of history— and then press the Tab key. Bash has figured out where you're going with this and completes it for you. Keep this one in mind, because there are many cases where it can easily save you dozens of keystrokes.

Finally, you won't survive long in the Linux world without becoming familiar with its built-in documentation. Type *man* (short for manual), followed by the name of a command.

```
man cat
```

The document that opens will list the basic purpose, function, and command-line arguments of the program you specified. If you're not sure of the exact spelling of the command, you can use apropos:

```
apropos zip
```

Apropos will return the names of all the man files that seem relevant to your search string. You can then access the file you're after using *man*.

Processing Text Streams

I'll be going through a lot of tools rather quickly now. But before I begin, I should note that some of them might at first seem a bit unnecessary—almost silly. It's good to remember that many of these won't normally be used directly on the command line the way you will here. Their true value might only become obvious to you once you deploy them as part of more complicated scripts designed to automate some system process.

I'll try to make things as realistic as possible, but your immediate goal should be to understand a command's function, and then store the information away somewhere in your brain from where it can be retrieved when necessary.

■ **Note**   With one or two exceptions, these tools, on their own, will have no effect on the files they access. They will read the text, transform it somehow, and then deploy it somewhere else. But the source file will usually remain as it was. You'll only see the simplest examples of each of these commands: their functionality will invariably extend much further. As always, don't forget that you absolutely MUST play with variations of every example on your own. It's the only way to learn.

Let's go.

You've already used cat to read files. But did you know that adding the -n flag lets you print to the screen with numbered lines?:

```
cat -n /etc/passwd
```

The nl command (nl stands for number lines) will produce exactly the same effect as cat -n.

Now that you've seen what the passwd file looks like when printed, take a good look at this use of the cut command:

```
cut -d: -f1 /etc/passwd
```

This reads the passwd file (which contains details of all existing user accounts). The -d flag sets the delimiter as colon (:), which means that, whenever a colon appears in the text, cut will think of it as the start of a new text field. The f1 means that you're only interested in printing the first field of every line. Try it yourself and note how you've printed just a single column of account names.

Expand and *unexpand* will convert tabs contained in text to spaces (expand) or spaces to tabs (unexpand):

```
expand -t 10 filename      # convert every tab to ten spaces.
unexpand -t 3 filename     # convert every three spaces to tabs.
```

You can use fmt to format the way text is printed to the screen:

```
fmt -w 60 filename         # start a new line after 60 characters.
fmt -t filename            # indent all but the first line of a paragraph
```

Another formatting tool is pr. Try this example:

```
pr -d -l 10 filename
```

The -d will add a new space in between lines (d = double space), and -l sets the maximum number of lines to print per screen. In this case, that's ten.

To print only a specified number of lines from a file, use head or, predictably, tail. A "line," by the way, is all the text to the left of a hard return. This is really meant for data files like logs whose lines are relatively short. If your file is broken down into paragraphs (like the ones on this page), then each complete *paragraph* will count as a single line.

```
head -10 filename # print only the first ten lines of a file.
tail -n 3 /etc/passwd # print only the last three lines of the passwd file.
```

Tail, with the -f flag, can also be used for ongoing monitoring of log files. In this example, tail will print any new entries to the syslog log file as they are added:

```
tail -f /var/log/syslog
```

You can use join to merge data from two files with overlapping columns. Here's the content of a file called column1:

1. New York

2. Chicago

3. Miami

4. Los Angeles

And here's the file column2:

1. New York

2. Illinois

3. Florida

4. California

Running join against both files like this:

```
join column1 column2
```

will output this handy list:

1. New York New York

2. Chicago Illinois

3. Miami Florida

4. Los Angeles California

If you'd like to create a new file using exactly the output of that join operation, you simply pipe the stream to the file name of your choice, like this:

```
join column1 column2 > newfilename
```

Paste is another tool for merging the contents of multiple files. Paste without any arguments will print two files, side by side:

```
paste column1 column2
```

Paste -s will print them sequentially:

```
paste -s column1 column2
```

You can rearrange the way lines in a file are displayed using *sort*. Without any arguments, sort will display the data in alphabetical sequence. Adding -r will reverse the order, -n will sort by number, rather than letter, and -nr will display the output in reverse numeric order:

```
sort /etc/passwd
sort -r /etc/passwd
sort -n /etc/passwd
cat -n /etc/passwd | sort -nr
```

There are more ways to control the lines that are printed, including uniq, which will print only lines that are unique to the file. Using uniq without any arguments will print only the first time a repeated line appears. Running it with the -u argument will only print lines that are never repeated. Create a file named text.txt with some contents and try it yourself:

```
uniq text.txt uniq -u text.txt
```

Using split will divide a single file into multiple files of a specified length. In this case, new files will actually be created while the original file remains unchanged:

```
split -2 filename
```

This will split the file into multiple files of two lines each, named xaa, xab, xac, and so on. Here too, "line" really means "paragraph."

An octal dump (od) will print text in various formats. Using od with no arguments:

```
od filename
```

will print the text in the octal data format (which will prove most exciting for our computers, but rather less so for us poor, illiterate humans). *od -a filename* will (among other things) substitute "ht" for tabs and "sp" for spaces. *od -c filename* will display tabs as \t and new lines (i.e., paragraphs) as \n.

You can transform text using tr. This command will convert all lowercase letters to uppercase:

```
cat /etc/passwd | tr "a-z" "A-Z"
```

If you need access to some basic document statistics, wc will output the total number of lines, words, and bytes in a specified text stream or file:

```
wc /etc/passwd
```

36

Finally, the LPI expects you to understand sed. The fact is, that sed—the Unix stream editor—is a science and an art wrapped up in a scripting tool. Very beautiful and complex things can be done with sed, and it would take far more space than I have available for you to appreciate that. Still, one simple example will have to do for our purposes right now.

The strength of sed is its ability to "filter text in a pipeline." This example takes input from a stream (via cat) and substitutes the word goodbye for the first occurrence on a line of hello:

```
cat text.txt | sed s/hello/"goodbye"/
```

Adding "g" (global) at the end will cause sed to replace every occurrence of hello on a line:

```
cat text.txt | sed s/hello/"goodbye"/g
```

File Management

For those of you who are used to managing your files and directories through colorful GUI programs that provide drag-and-drop edits and context-sensitive information with every right-click, the command line will, at first, seem a bit awkward. But once you've had some experience with a small handful of tools, you'll probably never want to go back. The speed and pinpoint accurately with which you can work with either entire filesystems or individual files through the command line—and the ability to do it on remote systems as easily as you would on your own PC—make this the first choice for just about anyone with the skills.

I will note one very big difference: when you delete a file using a GUI interface, the file is usually sent off to a trash can somewhere from which it can be restored. There are generally no second chances on the command line. Once it's gone, it's gone for good.

All set? Great. Let's get moving. You can copy files using cp:

```
cp myfile /home/myname/Desktop/
```

This will copy the file named myfile to the Desktop directory belonging to the myname user. If you're copying to a file that's outside your own account, you'll need to have root access:

```
sudo cp myfile /home/anothername/Desktop/
```

By adding the -r (recursive) argument, you can also copy subdirectories and their contents:

```
sudo cp -r /home/myname/mydirectory/ /usr/share/place/
```

This will copy everything that lives in or beneath the /mydirectory/ directory.

You create new directories with mkdir. Remember, creating directories outside your account requires root privileges. If you want to move the directory to within your current location, you can use a relative address:

```
mkdir newdir
```

If, on the other hand, the new directory will be somewhere else, you'll need to use its absolute address:

```
sudo mkdir /etc/newdir
```

If you need a nested hierarchy of directories, you add the -p (parents) flag and all the necessary directories will automatically be created:

```
sudo mkdir -p /etc/path/to/mydirectory/
```

This will create the /path/to/mydirectory/ directories (if necessary).

Copying files leaves the original source file where it was and creates a copy in a new location (or in the same directory but with a new name). *Moving* files deletes the source and re-creates it in a new location or with a new name:

```
mv myfile newname
mv myfile /home/myaccount/Desktop/
```

If you can copy and move files and directories, you should probably be able to delete them, too. In fact, rm will do just that:

```
rm myfile
```

Using rm -r newplace will remove the directory newplace (assuming that it's within your current directory location) and all the files it contains. Adding the -i argument makes the process interactive, meaning that you will be asked to confirm that this is what you actually want to do.

Besides rm -r, you can also delete empty directories using rmdir. Naturally, you can perform all of these operations on more than one file at a time using file name expansion (also known as globbing). Using the asterisk (*), for instance, will act on all the files in a directory:

```
rm -r *
```

Be very careful with that one: it will delete all files in this directory, along with all the subdirectories and their files that live beneath it!

Similarly:

```
rm file?
```

will delete all the files in the current directory with file names that include the word file and any single additional character. This would delete files named file1, file2, and files, but not file10. But typing:

```
rm file*
```

on the other hand, will delete files with file and any number of additional characters. This would, therefore, include file10.

You can list the contents of a directory using ls. And using ls -l will list the files and subdirectories in long form, displaying their file attributes and permissions. Using ls -a will display all files, even those classified as hidden, which are identified by a dot in front of their names. Using ls -lh will print file attributes, but with the file sizes displayed in human-friendly form, rather than in bytes.

Using touch will create a new, empty file:

```
touch newfile
```

Applying touch will also update the access-time metadata associated with a file.

Running the *file* command against a file will display file details:

```
file myfile
```

If you're into file management on an industrial scale, you'll need a tool that's everything cp and mv is, but much more. Does Linux have anything to offer? You betcha. It's called dd.

Now don't be frightened off by the fact that many admins believe dd stands for Disk Destroyer. Or, perhaps you should be frightened, because the tinniest of syntax errors in a dd operation can, indeed, result in the permanent loss of entire partitions' worth of data. So be frightened, but also, be prepared.

What makes dd different is that it sort of ignores your filesystem rules and limitations and makes perfect, exact copies of whatever you tell it to. The benefit of this is that you can ghost an entire disk, copy it to a completely new disk on a different computer, boot it, and it will run like it was born there.

■ **Note**   This obviously won't work for Windows disks because Microsoft, for all intents and purposes, chains their operating systems to the hardware they were originally installed on.

To copy a partition called sdb1 to a USB drive called partitionbackup, run this:

```
dd if=/dev/sdb1 of=/media/usb/partitionbackup
```

To copy an entire drive (called, say, sdb) to a backup drive called drivebackup that's mounted at /mnt/drive/ run:

```
dd if=/dev/sdb of=/mnt/drive/drivebackup
```

And don't forget to double and triple check your syntax and then offer a short prayer before hitting the Enter key.

File Archives

Whether it's automating backups, compressing files to save space, or transferring data between machines, at some point, you'll need to work with archive and compression software. The LPI expects you to be at least familiar with gzip and gunzip (which use the .gz extension), bzip2 (.bz2), and xz (.xz). Each of these offers some unique compression algorithm or feature not found in the others, but that's beyond the scope of this book. I will, however, discuss tar and cpio.

Normally, file names with the .tar extension (which, at one point at least, stood for Tape ARchive) are archives. That means there are at least two source files bundled together into a single archive file. If there's also a .gz extension (i.e., filename.tar.gz), then the archive is probably compressed. You don't have to use these extensions, but there are plenty of good reasons to stick to the accepted naming convention.

To create a tar archive of all the files in a particular directory, you use the c, v, and f command-line arguments:

```
tar cvf archivename.tar /home/myname/mydirectory/*
```

The first argument, c, means create, v tells tar to be verbose and print any necessary updates to the screen, and f points to the file you are creating. The f must always be the last argument and must be immediately followed by the name of the archive. The asterisk (*) after the source directory address tells tar to compress all files and subdirectories it finds in that directory.

If you also want to *compress* the archive, then you should add the letter z as an argument, and, if you decide to follow naming conventions, the .gz extension:

```
tar czvf archivename.tar.gz /home/myname/mydirectory/*
```

To decompress and extract the files of an archive into the current working directory, you use the x (extract) argument rather than c:

```
tar xzvf archivename.tar.gz
```

You can put tar to work on a data stream. This example (executed from the root directory) will use find to search down through four directory levels (-maxdepth 4) for files with names (-name) that include a .txt extension, and then pipe the file names through xargs (which allows command execution on streaming data) so that tar can create a new archive:

```
sudo find . -maxdepth 4 -name "*.txt" | xargs tar cvf textarch.tar
```

This is an excellent example of the way you can combine multiple Linux commands into a single line to generate, filter, and then act on data streams.

The cpio archive tool works primarily through piped data. So, for instance, you can feed it the output of an ls (list directory contents) command, and use that to create an archive (called myarchivename) of the files that are named:

```
ls | cpio -o > myarchivename.cpio
```

You can add compression via gzip:

```
ls | cpio -o | gzip > myarchivename.cpio.gz
```

Finally, this is how you would use cpio to create the same archive you built earlier using tar:

```
sudo find ./ -maxdepth 4 -name "*.txt" | cpio -o >
/home/ubuntu/archivename.cpio
```

Streams, Pipes, and Redirects

All Linux commands have three streams opened for them: stdin (Standard Input, which is identified numerically by a 0), stdout (Standard Output, 1), and stderr (Standard Error, 2). You can often access or redirect those streams by referencing their numeric representation. Here's a simple example:

```
tail -f /var/log/syslog 1> log-data.txt
```

This example will print all new entries to the syslog log file and pipe the standard output (1) to a file called log-data.txt. In truth, however, the default behavior of the > pipe is standard output, so the result would have been the same if you had used this syntax:

```
tail -f /var/log/syslog > log-data.txt
```

It's important to remember that using the > pipe will overwrite all data in the target file. In other words, had there already been a file called log-data.txt in that directory, all of its existing data would have been destroyed and replaced with whatever syslog sent its way. If you had wanted to append the new data (i.e., to add it to the end of the existing file), you would have used a double >> like this:

```
tail -f /var/log/syslog >> log-data.txt
```

You definitely don't want to forget this detail!

You can also redirect error messages. I'll give you a great example of why this might be useful in just a moment, but first, here's a simple illustration:

```
cat filename 2> errors.txt
```

This will stream the contents of the file called filename and, because I've used 2>, write any error messages (but NOT the file contents) to a file called errors.txt. If there is a file called filename, then errors.txt will be empty because there was no error to report. But if there is NO filename file, then error.txt. will contain a message that looks something like this:

```
cat: filename: No such file or directory
```

Now, why might you want to use this? Suppose you're using tar to compress and back up a drive with 50GB of data. This is going to take some time and will process thousands of individual files. You don't really want to have to sit staring at your screen watching for error messages, do you?

That's what I thought. Wouldn't it be nice if, instead, you could automatically redirect any error messages to a text file that you could read later at your leisure? Here's how that might look:

```
tar cvf newarchive.tar /dev/sdb1 2> error.txt
```

Don't think, by the way, that you're forced to choose only one place for your command output to go. Linux, caring for your overall happiness as deeply as it does, lets you have your cake and eat it too. By using *tee*, you can send streams to multiple targets. In this example, the ls -l output (stdout) will print to the screen as it normally would, while also populating a new file called lists.txt:

```
ls -l | tee list.txt
```

You can also make a second command conditional on the success of the first. This sequence will copy a file between remote locations and then delete the original copy *only if* the copy operation was successful:

```
scp filename myname@domain.com:/home/myname/ && rm filename
```

Running the same sequence with a semicolon (;) rather than double ampersands (&&) will delete the file *regardless* of the outcome of the first command.

```
scp filename myname@domain.com:/home/myname/ ; rm filename
```

Using a double pipe (‖) will run *either* the first *or* the second command, but not both. In this (rather silly) case, only if the copy was *unsuccessful*, will the original file be removed:

```
scp filename myname@domain.com:/home/myname/ || rm filename
```

Managing Processes

If you want to manage the processes running on your system, you'll first have to figure out exactly what they are. Worry not! Linux has you really well covered on that.

Monitoring Processes

Let's start with top:

```
top
```

Top launches an automatically updating table that displays a screen of information about the processes currently using the most system resources. This can be especially useful if you've noticed things slowing down and you want to find out what's behind it.

Top also allows you to see *who* is behind a particular process. This can be useful when choosing an appropriate course of action: you don't want to shut down the boss's Facebook session, do you?

You might also like to know how much of your RAM is in use and how much is still available. Running *free* will do that:

```
free
```

Adding the -h argument will display the result in easier-to-read megabytes or gigabytes.

To print a list of all processes to the screen, run the *ps* command:

```
ps
```

If you just tried this out for yourself (and I sincerely hope you did), you will probably be a bit disappointed. Your output will probably look something like this:

```
PID TTY            TIME CMD
9455 pts/7     00:00:00 bash
9861 pts/7     00:00:00 ps
```

If these are all the current processes, then it doesn't look like there's all that much happening right now, especially since the second entry is the ps command you just executed.

Let me clear something up. When I wrote that ps will display all processes, I meant all the processes being used by the *current shell*. But, in my example at least, the current shell has a PID (process ID) of 9455, meaning that there are as many as 9454 running processes higher up the chain that weren't displayed.

So what magic incantations will be needed before you're shown the whole collection? You could use either ps -e (using standard syntax) or ps aux (BSD syntax). Try both out to see the difference.

As mentioned earlier, you can always use grep to filter the output to a more manageable level:

```
ps aux | grep gnome-terminal
```

You can use pgrep to search for a PID by filtering by user or process name. This example will search for any instance of the sshd process being run by the root user:

```
pgrep -u root sshd
```

Managing Background Processes

One of the more obvious advantages of a GUI desktop experience is the ability to easily switch between programs. It's easy for newcomers to the terminal interface to feel imprisoned within their single terminal window. Once they launch a longer process—say, copying a very large file from one drive to another—there doesn't seem to be a way to get other work done until the copy operation is complete.

But it turns out that the restrictions are mostly imaginary. Let's experiment with an operation that will take some time. Let's say you want to copy a large video file. Starting the process normally will indeed keep control of your terminal:

```
cp filename.mp4 filename2.mp4
```

However, running the same command with an ampersand character added to the end will launch the process in the background:

```
cp filename.mp4 filename2.mp4 &
```

Now, while this is still running, type ps and see what you get:

```
PID TTY              TIME CMD
8750 pts/1     00:00:00 bash
11598 pts/1     00:00:00 cp
11599 pts/1     00:00:00 ps
```

You can see that the ps command took PID 11599 and the copy operation is 11598. Type *jobs* if you want to list all the processes currently running in the background of this shell. Note that this command will give you a different PID: this time it's the job number in relation to specifically this shell, which explains why you probably got the ID number of 1, rather than something in the high thousands. This is the ID you'll use to edit the job status. To bring this copy job back to the foreground, type:

```
fg 1
```

where fg stands for foreground, and 1 is the job number you got through *jobs*. To suspend the job, hit Ctrl+z. From there you can, if you like, restart the job and send it back to the background to complete, using:

```
bg 1
```

If you want to make sure that your background job finishes even if you should exit this shell, append nohup to the initial commands.

There's another way to juggle multiple processes in a terminal: GNU screen. Screen lets you multiplex terminal windows, effectively running more than one process out of a single terminal. You can even split a single screen into two windows. Screen is not installed by default in every Linux distribution, so you might have to get it:

```
sudo apt-get install screen
```

To launch the service, simply type *screen* from the command line. You'll be shown a page of introductory text, and then find yourself back at what looks like a regular command prompt. You can continue working as normal if you like, but you can also use various screen tools to orient yourself within the system and to move around. You use Ctrl+a key combinations for most functionality in screen:

```
CTRL+a w
```

which will print your current shell at the bottom of the screen. Using:

```
screen -ls
```

will list all currently open screens. You use screen -x and the PID from the list to rejoin a screen from your shell:

```
screen -x 12482
```

Assuming that 12482 is the PID of a valid screen, I will be returned to that shell. You can create and join a new window using Ctrl+a c. Ctrl+a S will split the screen horizontally to give you two shells in one terminal window. You can move between the shells using Ctrl+a tab. You can exit a screen using Ctrl+a \.

Killing Processes

So far you've learned how to monitor and manage processes. Now you'll have to see how to knock 'em off when they're no longer needed. But how do you know when they're no longer needed? One good indication is that they've stopped properly responding, but are still taking up system resources and are generally slowing everything else down.

If you know the PID of the offending process (perhaps by running top), you can use it with kill to bring it down:

```
kill 2934
```

If you know the name of the process, you can use killall:

```
killall process-name
```

If the process is owned by the system or even by the account belonging to a different user, you will need admin powers (sudo) to kill it.

By default, kill and killall will send sigterm (terminate signal), which is represented by the numeric value of 15. For a list of all signals and their values, type:

```
kill -l
```

Common signal codes you should be aware of include 1 (sighup—parent shell is closing), 2 sigint (interrupt—the same as Ctrl-c), 9 (shut down), and 15. The signal pkill works much like killall, but has the additional—and rather alarming—feature of attempting to silently guess at what you really meant with a misspelling.

Execution Priorities

Of all the colorful and sometimes downright fun names given to Linux processes, I'd vote for nice as the one that best illustrates what it does.

If your system hosts hundreds of resource-hungry programs all competing for the same memory or CPU cycles, you'll need a police officer on duty to make sure no one gets more than their fair share. On Linux, that police officer is called nice.

You can assign each process with its own nice value between 19 and -20, where 19 is very nice, and -20 is just plain nasty. A process with a nice value of 19 is so nice, that it will yield its rights to a finite resource to just about any other process asking for it. If, on the other hand, it's set to -20, a process will grab as much of the resource pie as it can, giving itself top priority. By default, most processes start with a neutral value of 0.

You can set a nondefault nice value by launching a program this way:

```
nice -10 apt-get install apache2
```

This will set the nice value to 10 (not negative 10), meaning it will, when possible, run when resource demand is generally low. A negative value is set this way:

```
nice --10 apt-get install apache2
```

If you know its PID, you can use renice to change the nice value of a process even once it's already running:

```
renice -10 -p 3745
```

With the -u argument, you can apply renice to all the processes associated with the named user:

```
renice 10 -u tony
```

Finally, you can also set the value for all processes owned by particular group:

```
renice 10 -g audio
```

Using Regular Expressions (REGEX)

You've already had a number of opportunities to see grep at work filtering text streams by specified strings. Now let's spend a bit of time on just how it interprets metacharacters. Despite your suspicion that grep got its name from the noise made by a strange swamp creature that lived in some Unix developer's backyard, it actually stands for Global Regular Expression Print. Which begs the question: just what is a Regular Expression (or REGEX)? For grep, all characters are REGEX except for those listed in Table 3-1.

Table 3-1. _Non-REGEX (Regular Expression) Characters_

Backslash	\
Caret	^
Dollar sign	$
Dot	.
Pipe symbol	|
Question mark	?
Asterisk	*
Plus sign	+
Parentheses	()
Square brackets	[]
Curly braces	{}

What this means in practical terms is that you shouldn't expect grep to interpret any one of those special characters as part of your plain-text string. Rather, each will be understood as a metacharacter. If you want grep to read any of these characters as regular text, you'll need to add a backslash to the left of the character to escape the metareading. Let's illustrate that. Suppose you had a file whose name, for some odd reason, was read(this)andthat. If you used grep to search your directory for all file names that include the string "(this":

```
ls | grep (this
```

you'd get an error:

```
bash: syntax error near unexpected token '('
```

That's because grep expected the (character to work according to its metameaning. However, if you would escape the (character in your search, like this:

```
ls | grep \(this
```

grep will successfully find the file for you. You can also enclose the entire string in quotation marks to get the same result:

```
ls | grep "(this"
```

While grep uses REGEX, its two cousins—egrep and fgrep—take different approaches: egrep (Extended grep, which should now be used as grep -E) has a larger list of characters it reads as metacharacters, while fgrep (grep -F) treats all characters as strictly literal and will often work more quickly as a result.

Using vi

The fact is that many admins go long periods of time between sessions with any one of the various flavors of the vi editor. I'm not exactly recommending that for you, but you should be aware of the alternatives and focus on whichever tool will best fit your needs.

Having said that, it would be hard to imagine a text processing tool that could come close to the efficiency and speed of vi in the hands of a master. Built at a time when the range of characters supported by many keyboards was far narrower than today, vi allowed you to do just about everything with the relatively small number of keys you had. Practically speaking, once you get used to this kind of focus, you can work very productively without ever having to move your fingers far. And don't even think about using a mouse.

So why would someone NOT want to use vi (or its more modern version: Vim)? For some, the time it takes to get used to the sometimes unintuitive controls makes Vim appear to be an expensive luxury. Those admins prefer to use more intuitive editing tools like Nano, or even a GUI editor like gedit. Whatever you use, just make sure that it saves your files as plain text. Never use a word processor like LibreOffice for administration tasks, as it will automatically add all kinds of invisible formatting.

In any case, vi is the text editor required by the LPIC exam, so here we go.

I'll discuss the more modern *Vim* version. Vim works in three different modes. When you first launch it (using either the vi or vim commands), you will find yourself in Normal (or Command) mode. By pressing the colon (:) key, you can switch to command-line mode to perform some basic file management operations. Table *3-2* lists the basic options when in command-line (or last line mode) mode.

Table 3-2. *Command-line Options in vi (or Vim)*

:w	Save the current file to disk (you will be prompted for the file name).
:w!	Overwrite the current file.
:exit	Write the current file and then close Vim.
:wq	Same as :exit.
:q	Close Vim without saving the current file.
:q!	If file has been changed but you don't want to save it, then
:e!	Walk back changes since last write.

Typing the letter "i" in Normal mode will take you to the third mode: Insert. While in Insert mode, you can use the Arrow keys to move your cursor through your document, and the alphanumeric keys to insert text wherever your cursor happens to be. For most of us, this mode is the most familiar of the three, but it's not where Vim experts get most of their work done.

That, believe it or not, is back in Normal mode (which you can reach from Insert mode by hitting the Esc key). Table *3-3* contains a summary of the keystroke combinations.

Table 3-3. *Vim Keystroke Commands in Normal Mode*

h	Moves the cursor left one character.
j	Moves the cursor down one line.
k	Moves the cursor up one line.
l	Moves the cursor right one character.
0	Moves the cursor to the start of the current line.
dw	Deletes the word that comes immediately after the cursor.
d$	Deletes from the insertion point to the end of the line.
dd	Deletes the entire current line.
D	Deletes the rest of the current line from the cursor position.
p	Inserts the text deleted in the last deletion operation after current cursor location
u	Undoes the last action.
yy	Copies the line in which the cursor is located to the buffer.
ZZ	Saves the current file and ends vi.
/	Search (for the term you enter)

Of course, none of this will be of much use to you if you don't open up a terminal, run Vim, and try it out. Perhaps you could open a (nonessential!) file that already has a few paragraphs of text that you can use to experiment.

Now Try This

Using only the command line, create a compressed archive (.tar.gz) of all the files and subdirectories in a busy directory on your computer, copy the archive to a different partition (perhaps to a USB drive), and extract it in its new home.

Extra credit if, using scp, you can copy the archive over a network to a remote computer. Extra extra credit if you can also (very carefully) do it using dd.

Test Yourself

1. What can the uname command display?

    a. Your login name

    b. Your most recent command

    c. The name of your OS

    d. The most recent variable you created

2. The .bash_history file contains:

   a. Your most recent commands

   b. The most recent variables you have used

   c. The most recent directories you have visited

   d. Documentation for the most recent program you used

3. Which of these will NOT change the number of characters displayed?

   a. cut -d: -f3 filename

   b. unexpand -t 5 filename

   c. head -10 filename

   d. fmt -w 60 filename

4. Which of these will create at least one new file?

   a. split -3 filename

   b. od filename

   c. join filename1 filename2

   d. wc /var/log/syslog

5. Which of these commands will copy subdirectories?

   a. cp -s /etc /dev/sdb1

   b. cp -r /etc /dev/sdb1

   c. cp -lh /etc /dev/sdb1

   d. cp -a /etc /dev/sdb1

6. Which of these will copy your root filesystem to a backup drive?

   a. dd if=/media/usb/backup/

   b. dd if=/root/ of=/media/usb/backup

   c. dd if=/ of=/home

   d. dd if=/ of=/media/usb/backup/

7. In which of these cases will a file called error.txt be created?

   a. Running cat filename 1> errors.txt when there is no such file

   b. Running cat filename 1> errors.txt when there is such a file

   c. Running cat filename 2> errors.txt when there is no such file

   d. Running cat filename 0> errors.txt when there is such a file

8. ls -l | tee list.txt will redirect traffic to which two places?

    a.   The screen and the file list.txt

    b.   The screen and an error file

    c.   List.txt and /var/log/syslog

    d.   The screen and /var/log/tee.log

9. Which of these will display all current system processes?

    a.   ps

    b.   ps -h

    c.   ps -e

    d.   ps aux

10. To return a process to the foreground, you use fg and the PID displayed by which command?

    a.   ps aux

    b.   job

    c.   bg

    d.   CTRL+z

11. Which of the following will close a screen in GNU Screen?

    a.   screen -x

    b.   screen x

    c.   CTRL-a w

    d.   CTRL+a \

12. Running kill with the value of 2 will send …

    a.   sigint

    b.   sighup

    c.   sigterm

    d.   pizza and beer

13. Which of these will create a nasty process?

    a.   nice -15 apt-get install apache2

    b.   renice 15 apt-get install apache2

    c.   nice --15 apt-get install apache2

    d.   nice --15 -g audio

14. Which of the following will interpret (hello) as plain text?

    a. grep

    b. grep -E

    c. grep -F

    d. egrep

15. Which of the following will remove an entire line in Vim Normal mode?

    a. dw

    b. D

    c. ZZ

    d. dd

Answer Key

1. c, 2. a, 3. d, 4. a, 5. b, 6. d, 7. c, 8. a, 9. c AND d 10. b, 11. d, 12. a, 13. c, 14. c, 15. d

CHAPTER 4

■ ■ ■

Topic 104: Devices, Linux Filesystems, and the Filesystem Hierarchy Standard

Properly booting, running, and securing your servers and PCs require well-designed and well-maintained partitions and filesystems. Partitions, as you've seen in previous chapters, are logically defined regions of a physical drive set aside for some particular use. Filesystems are structures used to organize files on a partition—or, for that matter, across multiple partitions—so that the files can be effectively accessed and secured.

This chapter will cover partitions and filesystems with a particular interest in making files as easily accessible as possible to those who need access, and beyond the reach of those who don't.

Create Partitions and Filesystems

Way, way back at the beginning of Chapter 1, I discussed how, during the boot process, your computer's firmware reads the Master Boot Record (MBR) on your boot drive. You remember all that stuff, right? Well good, because you're going to need it to understand how partitions can be managed—and rescued—in Linux.

The MBR architecture can support up to four partitions, of which one can be defined as secondary (the others must be primary). The secondary partition can be further subdivided into smaller partitions. You should be aware, however, that MBR is starting to show its age. For instance, it will only support drives up to 2TB in size.

■ **Note**   Two terabytes you say? Why the hard drive on my first computer back in the 1980s had only 10MB of space and that included the entire operating system. And you wouldn't believe how much serious work I got done back then! You kids today are all spoiled, that's what you are.

© David Clinton 2016
D. Clinton, *Practical LPIC-1 Linux Certification Study Guide*,
DOI 10.1007/978-1-4842-2358-1_4

Now that my obligatory "cranky-old-admin" rant is over, let's get back to business. Although I will add that that machine—an ITT XT—also had only 640K of RAM and smelled funny.

In any case, that 2TB ceiling is now starting to look rather low, and the shift to more modern systems is already well under way. The GPT (GUID Partition Table) is the most obvious choice. Among other things, you'll need it to allow dual booting with more modern versions of Windows.

To manage or troubleshoot uncooperative partitions, your first stop should probably be fdisk:

```
sudo fdisk /dev/sda
```

Typing m in the shell that opens will display a menu. Typing p will list your current partitions, which might look something like this:

```
Disk /dev/sda: 320.1 GB, 320072933376 bytes
255 heads, 63 sectors/track, 38913 cylinders, total 625142448 sectors
        Units = sectors of 1 * 512 = 512 bytes
        Sector size (logical/physical): 512 bytes / 512 bytes
        I/O size (minimum/optimal): 512 bytes / 512 bytes
        Disk identifier: 0x000163ac

Device Boot      Start         End      Blocks   Id  System
/dev/sda1   *      2048   620949503   310473728   83  Linux
/dev/sda2      620951550   625141759     2095105    5  Extended
/dev/sda5      620951552   625141759     2095104   82  Linux swap / Solaris
```

Notice the three partitions (sda1, sda2, and sda5) and the asterisk (*) in the Boot field of sda1, which identifies sda1 as the boot partition. It's also worth mentioning that a Linux partition type is identified by the number 83, Extended as 5, and Linux swap as 82.

If you want to create a new partition (after having carefully backed up all the data on the existing partitions, as this action can be destructive), you should hit n. You will be asked whether this partition should be primary or extended, and what its number and start and finish positions should be.

Don't think you're done at this point: there are still at least two steps to go. You should now hit t and select a partition type (82, 83, etc.). When you are absolutely sure that this is exactly what you want, you hold your breath and hit w to apply the changes.

If you launch fdisk against a GPT-formatted drive you will be politely told to go elsewhere for help:

```
sudo fdisk /dev/sdb
WARNING: GPT (GUID Partition Table) detected on '/dev/sdb'!
The util fdisk doesn't support GPT. Use GNU Parted
```

For this, you can use either parted, as advised:

```
sudo parted /dev/sdb
```

or gdisk, which follows much the same approach as fdisk, except for GPT partitions.

Now that you've got a new partition, you will still need to format it, or, in other words, apply the structure of a particular filesystem. You can use mkfs (which, obviously, stands for Make FileSystem) to format your partition, using the -t argument to specify a filesystem type:

```
sudo mkfs -t ext4 /dev/sdc1
```

Swap files, which allow disk space to be used to temporarily substitute for system memory (RAM), require a special tool:

```
sudo mkswap /dev/sdb2
```

And formatting to the reiserfs filesystem will work best with *its* own tool:

```
sudo mkreiserfs /dev/sdb1
```

As I've mentioned a number of different filesystems, let's briefly describe the most popular of them:

> **ext2** (extended): This filesystem offers no journaling. Journaling, by the way, means that a record of changes to a partition is saved to a journal to improve crash recovery.
>
> **ext3** and **ext4:** Both offer journaling, while ext4 also handles files up to 16TB. I think it's safe to say that ext4 is currently the most popular Linux filesystem, in fact, as of Linux kernel 4.3, the ext3 module has been removed.
>
> **reiserfs**: Both journaled and stable.
>
> **btrfs**: Known to be extremely stable and reliable.
>
> **XFS**: A 64-bit journaled filesystem that is particularly well suited to large files and filesystems.
>
> **VFAT**: An extension of the FAT32 filesystem. You may want to format removable media (like USB drives) to VFAT due to its compatibility with Windows.

Maintain the Integrity of Filesystems

The proper care and feeding of your happy filesystem requires you to focus on three areas: monitoring, preventative maintenance, and repair.

Monitoring

There's a lot you can learn about your infrastructure from carefully watching the size consumed by your data. For instance, once the files on a partition take up nearly all available space, you could see a significant drop in system responsiveness as the filesystem struggles to find space for everything.

Linux lets you keep an eye on things from a number of different perspectives and at various detail levels. Typing df will show you all the partitions—both physical and virtual—on your system, along with both their used and available space. Adding the -h argument will, as you've seen before, display the output in human readable terms:

```
df -h
```

The -i argument will display usage by inode. Inodes are data structures containing attributes and the disk block location of a file or directory. It is theoretically possible (although uncommon) that you could run out of available inodes while still having actual space left on your partition, so it's worth keeping this metric in mind (next to tonight's dinner menu and the dentist appointment you've got next Tuesday).

```
df -i
```

The du command will tell you how much disk space is being used by the contents of a specific directory or directory hierarchy (measured in kilobytes, by default). This can be useful when you're trying to track down exactly who has been using up all your partition space.

```
du
```

Adding -s will output only the total size.

```
du -s
```

There are some very creative and valuable uses for du, so make sure to read the man page.

```
man du
```

For a more detailed look into the inner workings of an ext partition, use dumpe2fs:

```
sudo dumpe2fs /dev/sdb2 | less
```

Because dumpe2fs will throw so much information at you, it's worthwhile piping it to *less* so you can read it one screen at a time.

Preventive Maintenance

It's always a nice idea to try to get a little control over your life *before* things go flying off into total chaos. So the tune2fs tool can be worth a look. You can use tune2fs to set the maximum number of disk mounts and the maximum interval (assuming you haven't hit the mount limit yet) between system checks:

```
sudo tune2fs -c 40 -i 1m /dev/sda1
```

The *-c 40* sets the maximum mounts between checks of the /dev/sda1 partition to 40, and *-i 1m* sets the interval to one month. If you're running an ext2 formatted disk and you're worried that you might face some crashes, you can add a journal, effectively converting the partition to ext3, using tune2fs –j:

```
sudo tune2fs -j /dev/sda1
```

And while I'm on the topic of tune2fs, I will mention that you can edit or add the filesystem volume label, which can make positively identifying a partition a lot more straightforward (and thereby help prevent accidents):

```
sudo tune2fs -L new_name /dev/sda1
```

Naturally, there are similar tools for other filesystems that work pretty much the same way.

Repair

So everything is collapsing all around you and getting home in time for supper is not even a possibility. Even breakfast is beginning to look a bit unlikely. Yes, the electrical cable is plugged in and both the front and rear power switches are on.

Assuming that the problem revolves around your inability to access data on the disk, you should first make sure that the drive is actually alive—if it's a hard disk drive, listen, or, if you're properly grounded, feel it to see if it's actually spinning. If it passes that test, here's what comes next.

57

If the drive is still mounted, unmount it (this assumes, of course, that you're running the system itself from a separate drive):

```
sudo umount /dev/sdc
```

Then run fsck (which stands for FileSystem ChecK):

```
sudo fsck /dev/sdc1
```

You might get a message like this:

```
Dirty bit is set. Fs was not properly unmounted and some data may be
corrupt.
```

This might be an indication that a corresponding block of memory has been changed but not yet saved to disk. It might suggest the presence of corrupted data. It's safe to let fsck remove it.

The e2fsck tool can also be called in for help. Running it against a device with -p will launch an automated, noninteractive repair action:

```
e2fsck -p /dev/sda1
```

Table 4-1 lists some alternate arguments for e2fsck.

Table 4-1. *e2fsck Command-line Arguments and Their Explanations*

-n	Make no changes to the filesystem
-y	Assume "yes" to all questions
-c	Check for bad blocks and add them to the badblock list
-f	Force checking even if filesystem is marked clean
-v	Be verbose
-b superblock	Use alternative superblock
-B blocksize	Force blocksize when looking for superblock
-j external_journal	Set location of the external journal
-l bad_blocks_file	Add to badblocks list
-L bad_blocks_file	Set badblocks list

Finally, running debugfs against a device like this:

```
sudo debugfs /dev/sda1
```

will drop you into a new shell where the question mark (?) will open a helpful menu.

Control Mounting and Unmounting of Filesystems

I just briefly mentioned unmounting a drive earlier, but I should probably spend a bit more time on the subject now. A physical drive might be attached to your PC and powered up, but it won't be accessible to a filesystem until it's been associated with an appropriate mount point. For most devices, this will normally happen automatically through entries in the /etc/fstab file. But you may sometimes have to manually mount or unmount a disk.

Traditionally, you usually mount devices to directories in /mnt or /media. In truth, however, you can actually use any location you like. Let's walk through the mount process. From inside the /media directory, use mkdir to create a new directory called newdrive:

```
sudo mkdir newdrive
```

Just to be absolutely sure, cd into the directory and run ls to confirm that it's empty:

```
cd /media/newdrive
ls
```

Now cd back up to the parent directory (/media, in this example):

```
cd ..
```

You will now need the name of the device you want to mount. Let's run lsblk to list all the block devices currently plugged in:

```
lsblk
```

Let's assume that /dev/sdc1 was the drive you're after. Now let's run mount to mount that drive to the newdrive directory:

```
sudo mount /dev/sdc1 /media/newdrive
```

Let's go in and take another look around:

```
cd newdrive
ls
```

You should be able to see all the files and directories that came with that drive, displayed inside the /media/newdrive directory.

When it's time to clean up your toys, you can use umount (without the first "n") to unmount the drive:

```
sudo umount /dev/sdc1
```

Sometimes you will try to mount a device but receive an "unknown type" error message. In this case, you will have to specify the filesystem type as part of your mount command:

```
sudo mount -t ext3 /dev/sdc1 newdrive
```

If you're not sure which type it is, you can try running mount with -a and it will attempt to mount the drive using all types.

Now, what about that fstab file? If you want a partition to load automatically at boot, you'll need to make sure that it has an entry in the plain text /etc/fstab file. Let's take a look at this example:

```
      cat /etc/fstab
# <file system> <mount point>      <type>    <options>
<dump> <pass>
# / was on /dev/sda2 during installation
UUID=d334de16-3d76-460f-a65e-2b35a6b763ba                 /
ext4    errors=remount-ro 0       1
# /boot/efi was on /dev/sda1 during installation
UUID=3613-9EDB   /boot/efi       vfat      defaults       0
1
# swap was on /dev/sda3 during installation
UUID=503d9513-257b-5622-9e15-c28ae8e504c3                 none
swap    sw              0      0
# old backup drive
UUID="0bc97b1d-f202-46a0-9514-dc860f0afa38"      /media/drive-
backup      ext4
```

Look at the fourth entry: "old backup drive." This one was added manually. To do that I needed to run the blkid program to retrieve the drive's UUID:

```
blkid /dev/sda1
```

Running blkid also told me that the partition was formatted to ext4. All that was left was to edit the fstab file and add a new line with the ID in quotation marks following UUID=, the mount point ("/media/drive-backup" in this case), and the file type (ext4). The next time the computer boots (or whenever *sudo mount -a* is run) the device will be accessible.

Manage Disk Quotas

Since data bloat can have such a serious impact on system behavior (not to mention use up space that might be needed for other processes and users), Linux allows you to assign quotas that limit the disk space and number of inodes a particular user or group can use. Appropriately enough, the program is called quota. You might need to install it, as it doesn't come with every fresh install.

This will install quota on a Fedora/CentOS/RHEL system:

```
sudo yum install quota
```

You'll need to add this text to the /etc/fstab entry of each drive you'd like quota to control:

```
,usrquota,grpquota
```

Now, you can either reboot the computer, or run:

```
sudo mount -a
```

to enable the new setting. You now need to build a table containing the current disk usage, update disk quota files, and create the aquota.group and aquota.user files. All that will be done by running:

```
sudo quotacheck -avmug
```

Here, a will check all, m will force a check on mounted filesystems, u and g will check users and groups, respectively, and v means verbose. Now you will need to actually turn quota on:

```
sudo quotaon -av
```

You can generate a quota report using, you guessed it, repquota:

```
sudo repquota -av
```

Out of the box, none of your users will actually have any restrictions, so you'll need to edit the settings. You run the edquota program to do that. To edit a user's quota, run:

```
sudo edquota -u <username>
```

To edit a group's quota, go with -g:

```
edquota -g <groupname>
```

Either way, edquota will open in vi (aren't you glad you played around with it as much as you did). You will see that you are able to control disk usage by either blocks or inodes, and apply either soft or hard limits. A soft limit will send a warning once a user exceeds his limit, but nevertheless permit him to continue using the space. A hard limit will prevent all exceptions to the rules. You can set the soft limit (and its maximum time) with the -t flag:

```
sudo edquota -t
```

Manage File Permissions and Ownership

Besides passwords and other user login control features, the most fundamental Linux tool for managing access to private and system resources is permissions.

Every object within a Linux filesystem has an owner and a group, and a set of rules that determine exactly who and what gets access. Somehow, three separate notational systems were developed to represent these permissions, and I'll explore all of them. They are Letters, Subjects, and Numbers.

Letters

Letters are divided into three uses, as shown in Table 4-2.

Table 4-2. *Letters Used in the Linux System*

Code	Permission
r	Read
W	Write
X	Execute

The subjects of these permissions are also divided into three groups, as shown in Table 4-3.

Table 4-3. *Subjects Used in the Linux System*

Code	Subject
u	User (the object owner)
g	Group
o	Other (all other users)

Therefore, if, say, you would want to add write permissions over a file for all users, you would run chmod like this:

```
chmod o+w myfile.txt
```

Here's how you would *remove* read permissions from members of the file's group:

```
chmod g-r myfile.txt
```

If you run ls -l against a particular file, you will see this represented graphically (well, as graphically as the Linux command line gets anyway):

```
ls -l | grep myfile
-rw--r--r-- 1 ubuntu ubuntu     0 Dec 15 18:17 myfile.txt
```

The first group of characters (-rw) tells you that the user (named ubuntu, in this case) has both read and write permissions. Thanks to the g-w operation before, the group (also called ubuntu) has only read but not write authority, as do all others. If this object were a directory rather than a file, the first character in the line would be the letter d.

You can use chown to change an object's owner and group. Let's transfer ownership of this file over to Steve. Because there's more than one owner involved here, you'll need root powers to do this:

```
sudo chown steve:steve myfile.txt
```

The second "steve" defines the group the object belongs to (in this case, the group called "steve"). If you wanted to change ownership of a directory *and* its contents (and subdirectories), you would add -R:

```
sudo chown -R steve:steve /var/log
```

By the way, I definitely would not do this on a live system, as it would almost certainly mess up your logs!

Numbers (octal)

Numbers used in Linux system are also divided into three groups, as shown in Table 4-4.

Table 4-4. *Numbers Used in the Linux System*

Value	Permission
4	Read
2	Write
1	Execute

You can use these numbers with chmod to achieve exactly the same effect as r, w, and x. To configure a file's permissions to allow read and write powers to the user and group, but only read to others, run this:

```
chmod 664 myfile.txt
```

What's going on here? Well, the values of read (4) and write (2), would, when added together, come to 6. So you assign the number 6 to the first two positions (user and group). The third position represents "others," so you'll give that the number 4, read only.
    Let's try another one:

```
cd /bin
ls -l | grep cp
-rwxr-xr-x 1 root root    130304 Mar 24    2014 cp
```

The cp binary file depicted here would have an octal value of 751. Why? Well, it gives rwx (read/write/execute; 4+2+1=7) to the user, r-x (read/execute; 4+1=5) to the group, and x (execute; 1) to others.

Umask

The third representational system, umask, is a bit of a funny creature. It represents an inversion of an object's permissions. In other words, if the normal octal representation of an object is 751, its umask would be 0026. Ignoring the first digit, the second 0 comes from subtracting 7 (the object's "user" value) from 7 (the highest possible octal value). The 2 of the group is derived by subtracting 5 (the object's "group" value) from 7. And the 6 is what happens when you subtract 1 (executable) from 7.

One more example. The 664 you applied to myfile.txt above would have a umask of 0113. Work it out for yourself.

What is the umask used for? Type umask on the command line and see what you get:

```
umask
```

The odds are that you saw 0002. What this means is that whenever the current user creates a new Linux object, it will automatically be given the value of 0002, or, in other terms, 664 (assuming it's a file that can't be executed). You can try it yourself by creating a file and then checking out its permissions:

```
touch newerfile.txt
```

You can edit your umask value (to change the permissions that new files will get) using something like:

```
umask 022
```

To prove it worked, create a new file:

```
touch newestfile.txt
```

and compare the permissions for both of them:

```
ls -l | grep newe
```

Know, however, that your umask value will only remain in effect until you close this particular shell (even though the permission settings of the files you created in the shell will be persistent).

Using suid, sgid, and the Sticky Bit

Sometimes you will want to restrict authority over a resource to as few people as possible, but nevertheless make it generally available in limited circumstances. The best example is passwd. The /etc/passwd file contains account information for all users on a Linux system, but it must also be accessed when individual users update account details like their passwords. So how can you maintain some control over such an important resource, while still allowing any user to access it for his own needs? By adding an suid (Set owner User ID), of course.

The suid elevates any user who *executes* the file to the status of owner for only as long as he is still executing. Let's take a look at the passwd file:

```
cd /usr/bin
ls -l | grep passwd
-rwsr-sr-x 1 root     root         47032 Feb 16    2014 passwd
```

Notice the rws rather than rwx? That's the suid. You can add the suid to an executable file using u+s:

```
sudo chmod u+s myexecutable
```

You can do pretty much the same thing for groups, meaning that when the *sgid* is set for a file, the process will have the same *group* rights as the file being executed. Using:

```
sudo chmod g+s yourexecutable
```

will add an sgid to this file, but only for members of its group. When sgid is applied to a directory, all files and subdirectories subsequently created will inherit the same group ownership from the parent directory.

You can apply a sticky bit to a directory to protect files within the directory from being deleted by other users (even users with file access). Let's create a new directory, check out its ls -l output, add the sticky bit (using -t), and then run ls -l once again to confirm:

```
sudo mkdir /run/ourfiles
cd /run
ls -l | grep ourfiles
sudo chmod +t ourfiles
ls -l | grep ourfiles
```

Create and Change Hard and Symbolic Links

Here's something to ponder: besides the many thousands of system files spread through hundreds of nested directories, let's image that your home directory hierarchy, like mine, holds more than 120,000 files. If you've done a good job arranging your directories so that you can quickly drill down and find most of what you're looking for—at least most of the time—then you're in pretty good shape.

But even if you know where a file is, if you need to access it often, plowing through all those layers of directories each time can be a real pain. You could simply move the file to wherever you are when you normally need it, but that might take it out of the environment where it will be backed up or updated. And who knows where you'll be the next time you need it?

So what's a poor admin to do? Link it.

Linux will let you place a symbolic copy of a file just about anywhere, so that executing or opening it in its new location will have exactly the same effect as opening it where it really lives.

There are two kinds of linked files: symbolic (or soft) links and hard links. Hard links are two files that actually share an inode, meaning that, although they may appear in different directories, they're actually the very same file.

You create a hard link using ln. Let's make a link in a directory called /home/ myname/files for the /home/myname/stuff1.txt file:

```
ln ~/stuff1.txt ~/files/
```

You can head over to the ~/files directory to take a look at your new identical twin. Make a change to one of the files and then quickly run back to the other to marvel at the miracle of synchronicity.

You create a symbolic (soft) link using ln -s. This example will create a symbolic link in your home directory to the cp (copy) file that lives in the /bin directory:

```
ls -s /bin/cp ~/
```

Run ls in both directories to compare the two:

```
ls -l
```

Here's an example of symlinked files. The binary that runs vi is in the /usr/bin directory. If you were to take a look at it:

```
ls -l /usr/bin/vi
lrwxrwxrwx 1 root root 20 Apr 6 2014 /usr/bin/vi ->
/etc/alternatives/vi
```

you would see the letter l (for link) at the beginning of the attributes, and an arrow pointing to /etc/alternatives. Let's take a look over there:

```
ls -l /etc/alternatives/vi
lrwxrwxrwx 1 root root 18 Apr 6 2014 /etc/alternatives/vi ->
/usr/bin/vim.basic
```

You can see the same attributes and an arrow pointing back to /usr/bin.

Find System Files and Place Files in the Correct Location

For those important files that aren't conveniently linked (or for those links that you've inconveniently lost), you'll need some other tools for finding things. Right now I am going to discuss some really powerful Linux tools. The first might not seem like a tool at all: the Linux Filesystem Hierarchy Standard (FHS).

Filesystem Hierarchy Standard

With some minor exceptions, Linux distributions stick to the FHS to define a common layout for pretty much all their system files. If you're familiar with the basic layout and purpose of just a half a dozen or so directories, then you're a step closer to finding just about anything.

Let's move to the root directory and list its contents:

```
cd /
ls
```

Of the directories that you can see, I'll focus on those listed in Table 4-5.

Table 4-5. *Key Directories in the Linux Filesystem Hierarchy Standard*

/bin	Core system executables and shells
/dev	Hardware devices
/etc	Text-based config files
/home	User home subdirectories. Your home directory will be /home/yourname/ and your Desktop, Downloads, and other directories will be in /home/yourname/
/lib	Code libraries
/usr	Application files
/var	Variable data including logs

That's it. Get a picture in your mind of those seven directories and their uses, and you're in business. Besides those, you should also be aware of some more directories listed in Table 4-6 (many of which were mentioned previously in this book).

Table 4-6. *Other Common Directories Found in the Linux Filesystem Hierarchy Standard*

/boot	Bootloader files
/media	Place to mount external devices
/mnt	Alternative location for mounting external devices
/opt	Program installation files
/proc	Pseudo filesystem representing processes
/root	Root user's home directory
/run	Runtime data storage
/sbin	Admin binaries
/srv	Site-specific data
/sys	System hardware info
/tmp	Temp system files

Search Tools

If, somehow, your new mental superpowers fail you and there's something you still can't find, you'll need to bring in the heavy guns. Suppose you want to find and list all the files in /etc/ with the .conf extension (hint: there are more than 600 on my Ubuntu system). Here you go:

```
sudo find /etc/ -name *.conf
```

The -name flag tells find to search for file names. (You need to be sudo or you'll be prevented from reading through certain directories.)

But that was too easy: you cheated by allowing *find* to narrow the search to the /etc/ directory. Let's try something a bit harder. Perhaps you've forgotten where the fstab file is kept:

```
sudo find / -name fstab
```

This did the job, but it took a bit longer because it had to search through all the files on the computer. Let's try something else:

```
locate fstab
```

Did you notice how much faster that went? How was *locate* able to pull that one off? Locate relies on an index of file names and locations that's updated regularly, so it doesn't need to crawl through every directory the way find does, it just needs to lazily browse its index. You can manually update the index using:

```
sudo updatedb
```

Locate behavior is defined in the /etc/updatedb.conf file.

If you know the name of a binary program, you can use some simple command-line tools to help you locate the actual binary file. Typing:

```
whereis ls
```

will display the location of the binary that runs the ls command, along with that of its source code and man file. Incidentally, running whereis with the -bms flag will accomplish the same thing (and get you that much closer to carpal tunnel syndrome in the process).

Typing *which* will return just the binary location, and typing *type* will identify any aliases associated with the binary:

```
which ls
type ls
```

Now Try This

Practice mounting and unmounting a USB drive to various locations on your filesystem (/media/newdirectory/ /mnt/newdirectory/ etc.). Now, after you've carefully ensured that the drive contains no important files, confirm its designation (/dev/sdb, /dev/sdc) and create a new ext4 partition out of all or, if you prefer, part of the drive. Then copy some files from your system to the new partition and use chown to edit the files' owner and chmod to make them readable by anyone.

Test Yourself

1. Which of the following filesystems is NOT journaled:

   a. ext3

   b. XFS

   c. ext2

   d. reiserfs

2. What will selecting "p" accomplish in fdisk?

   a. List current partitions

   b. List menu options

   c. Fix a corrupted partition

   d. Convert the partition to swap

3. Which of the following commands will display the total size taken up by specified directories and their files?

   a. df -i

   b. e2fsck -B

   c. du

   d. du -s

4. Which of these will successfully mount the drive called sdc1?

   a. sudo mount newdrive /dev/sdc1

   b. sudo mount /dev/sdc1 newdrive

   c. sudo /dev/sdc1 mount newdrive

   d. sudo mount sdc1 newdrive

5. **To which file must you add ,usrquota,grpquota to ensure quota will run?**

   a. /etc/fstab

   b. aquota.group

   c. edquota

   d. repquota

6. What is the correct octal value of a text file that was created by a user with the umask 0022?

   a. 641

   b. 644

   c. 664

   d. 422

7. What is the octal value that corresponds to -rwxrw-r--?

   a. 554

   b. 777

   c. 764

   d. 467

8. You create a symbolic link of the cp binary file using:

   a. ls -s /bin/cp ~/

   b. ls -s ~/ /bin/cp

    c.   ls /bin/cp ~/

    d.   ls ~/ /bin/cp

9.   Which of the following directories contains text-based config files?

    a.   /proc

    b.   /lib

    c.   /etc

    d.   /dev

10.   Which of the following will find the location of any file the quickest?

    a.   find

    b.   locatedb

    c.   locate

    d.   whereis

Answer Key

1. c, 2. a, 3. d, 4. b, 5. a, 6. b, 7. c, 8. a, 9. c, 10. c

CHAPTER 5

■ ■ ■

Topic 105: Shells, Scripting, and Databases

With this chapter, I'll reach the first material that falls under the LPIC-1 102 exam—the second of two exams required for the Linux Professional Institute's Linux Server Professional certification. If you're using this book as a guide to prepare for the exams, there's a good chance that you've just passed the 101 exam. Congratulations! If not, keep plugging away, you'll get there. And if you're not going after any certifications, but you just want to learn the IT skills you'll need to get by in the 21st century, then welcome: it's great to have you here.

Let's get started.

Customize and Use the Shell Environment

In the Linux world, a shell is a program that interprets what you type at the command line and relays it to the host operating system so it can be processed. There are a number of shell flavors (bash, dash, sh, etc.), each with its own distinct properties and default environment variables.

Whichever shell you choose, you can launch it in one of two ways: login and non-login. A non-login shell is one that launches from within a GUI desktop session (and, thus, requires no log in). Any remote or non-GUI session will require authentication and is therefore called a login session.

It's very important to be aware of this distinction, because the environment parameters of login vs. non-login shell sessions are controlled through different files. Why should you care? Because you will sometimes need to edit your parameters, something that will prove a whole lot harder if you can't find the right configuration file!

When a login shell launches, it will read the /etc/profile file first. Whether or not /etc/profile exists, the shell will then read the first of ~/.bash_profile, ~/.bash_login, or ~/.profile it finds. The shell will load with whatever values it finds.

■ **Note**   Using ~/, by the way, indicates a file in the user's own home directory. The dot preceding the file names means that these files are hidden—they are only visible to ls if the -a argument is added.

Non-login sessions will read the /etc/bash.bashrc and then the ~/.bashrc files. Unfortunately, you're just going to have to remember this.

If you need to change shell environments in the middle of a session, you can use the dot command. I kid you not: there's actually a command called dot:

```
. .bashrc
```

which, in this case, will switch to the bash shell.

You should also be aware of two more session-related items: ~/.bash_logout controls the way a shell session will close, including how anything left in memory is (or is not) erased. And any contents found in the /etc/skel/ directory will be automatically copied to the home directories of newly created users. This is a good way to automate the customized creation of new accounts. By default, desktop installations of Linux will usually place an examples.desktop file in /etc/skel/ that will add a directory structure (Desktop, Downloads, Documents) to new GUI accounts.

Another reason the shell configuration files are so important is that they will store new environment variables that you might create, making them available whenever you log in. One class of variable is called an alias. You can create an alias using the *alias* command (but I'll bet you already knew that):

```
alias prtz="cd /etc/;cat timezone"
```

This command will create a new alias called prtz (print time zone) and define it to perform two commands: *cd /etc/* and *cat timezone* (the timezone file contains nothing but your system's local time zone setting). Now, I'll admit that this particular example won't end up saving you all that many keystrokes, but you get the idea: rather than having to type out a long sequence of commands, you can get the job done with a short and easily remembered phrase.

You can remove an alias using unalias:

```
unalias prtz
```

Functions are slightly more complicated shell variables. In fact, they begin to approach scripts in their range. This one-line set up will create a function to list the contents of a directory that will be provided at runtime:

```
function listd() { ls -l $1; }
```

In this case, typing listd at the command line, along with the location of the directory you'd like displayed, will generate the list you're after:

```
listd /var/log
```

Functions, just like aliases, can be easily removed:

```
unset -f listd
```

Customize and Write Simple Scripts

Now that you've seen how you can "program" processes into newly created commands like alias and function, you're ready for shell scripts. Scripts lie somewhere between the command line and full programming and, in fact, share some stronger qualities with each.

Like the command line, scripts have full access to all Linux operations: you can manipulate files and system settings and work with text streams just as if you were at the command line. But you can also create much more complex data flows and abstractions with scripts that closely resemble many of the most flexible features of many programming languages.

The basic structure of a shell script is quite simple. The plain text file—often using an .sh extension in its name—will always begin with what's known as the shebang line, that identifies the binary of the particular shell you want to use (bash, in this case). Don't ask me why it's called shebang, by the way, I haven't a clue.

```
#!/bin/bash
```

That line will be followed by regular shell commands, comments (which aren't read by the shell when preceded by #), and, often, a final exit line:

```
#!/bin/bash
# this shell will print all directory files and then email it
# to the root account:
ls -l
# this line will return an exit code 0, which means "success":
exit 0
```

When you're ready to run the script, you simply launch it from the command line (while in the same directory) using:

```
./scriptname.sh
```

Not so fast there, Pilgrim. If you just tried that (and I surely hope you did), then you probably encountered this error message:

```
bash: ./scriptname.sh: Permission denied
```

Permission denied? But if you just created that file, aren't you automatically its owner? Why would you need permission?

The problem is that you haven't made the script executable, so Linux thinks that it's still a regular text file. That's easily fixed:

```
chmod +x scriptname.sh
```

Now you're ready to run it.

While you're there, I should explain how you can send the output of a script as an e-mail. Assuming the mail-utils package is installed on your system, piping a command to the mail program, which you can tell to generate an e-mail to the root user, will get that job done:

```
ls -l | mail -s "output of script" root
```

Let's work through some more examples to illustrate the main scripting functions.

User Inputs

You can incorporate user inputs into your scripts using variables introduced with the dollar sign ($) character. If you're familiar with programming, you will know that other languages require that you declare string variables before calling them. That's not necessary for bash scripts (although, as you will soon see, it is required if you want to use variables as integers).

In this case, you will echo a greeting message, use read to save the input as a value for the variable $answer (although you won't actually do anything with it in this example), and run the *date* command:

```
#!/bin/bash
echo "Type any character if you'd like to know the time"
read answer
echo "Ok, it's "
date
```

So now let's try importing and then working with integers:

```
!/bin/bash
declare -i number1
declare -i number2
declare -i total
echo "Please enter a number "
read number1
echo "And another number "
```

```
read number2 total=$number1+$number2
echo "Aha! They equal " $total
exit 0
```

What happened here? You first declared three variables (one for each input number and a third for the total that you will produce) and then, once again, used echo to ask the user for some input. This time, the values created by *read* are used to feed the sum of number1+number2 to the variable $total, which can then be printed to the screen as part of the echo line. Note how you only add the $ symbol to variable names when they are retrieved.

Testing Values

You can use various testing tools in your scripts to confirm the status of specified values at runtime. This can add a level of reliability to a script, as it makes it much less likely to fail due to information that wasn't available until runtime. In this example, -e will test for the existence of a resource (a directory, in this case), and *it* will launch an operation (adding that directory to the system PATH) if -e returns a positive result:

```
#!/bin/bash
echo "What directory do you want to add to the PATH?"
read NewPath
# -e will test for the existence of the new path
if [ -e "$NewPath" ]; then
    echo "The " $NewPath " directory exists."
    echo $NewPath " is now in the PATH."
    PATH=$PATH:$NewPath
    export PATH
    echo "Your PATH environment variable is now:"
    echo $PATH
else
    echo "Sorry, I'm afraid that " $NewPath " doesn't exist."
fi
exit 0
```

Notice that the structure of the if/else pair allows for a graceful failure should the resource not exist. Notice also the fi that closes the if/else pair; fi is, of course, if backward.

Besides -e, -f will confirm that a file exists *and* that it's a regular file, -d will confirm that a target is a directory (and not a file), and -r will confirm that a file is readable for the current user.

Another kind of test involves comparing multiple values to each other. This example will compare the values of text1 and text2 to test whether they're the same:

```
#!/bin/bash
echo "Please enter some text "
read text1
```

```
echo "Please enter some more text "
read text2
if test $text1 != $text2; then
        echo "they're not identical"
else
        echo "they are identical"
fi
exit 0
```

In the above example, != means "does **NOT** equal". You can also test using eq (does equal), lt (less than), and gt (greater than).

For those times when you are faced with more than two choices, if/else structures won't help. But the *case* structure most definitely will! This example will take the user input and apply it to three possible cases (each, through the use of the pipe [|] character, incorporating two choices). Be careful to get all the fine syntax details right. Also, note that esac is case in reverse.

```
#!/bin/bash
#A simple script to demonstrate the case structure.
echo "What's your favorite car?"
read CAR
case $CAR in
volvo | ford ) echo "Nice! I love" $CAR
;;
porsche | vw ) echo "Not bad..." $CAR"'s are ok, too"
;;
yugo | fiat ) echo "Yuk!" $CAR"'s are ugly"
;;
* ) echo "Sorry, I'm not familiar with that make!"
;;
esac
exit 0
```

Loops

Many scripts require repeated actions while—or until—a certain condition is met. You might, for example, want a script to launch some process only after a preceding process has completed. You could write a script to test for the existence of the first process so that, when the test fails, the new process is started.

Like anything else related to scripting, there really is no end to the possible scenarios a fertile imagination can dream up. Unfortunately, to illustrate the principles, you'll have to come back to my silly and unimaginative examples.

Here's a loop that, using *while*, will continue as long as a variable called COUNTER—set to start at 10 and reduced one integer at a time—remains higher than 2. Try it for yourself:

```
#!/bin/bash
#example of while loop:
declare -i COUNTER
COUNTER=10
    while [  $COUNTER -gt 2 ]; do
            echo The counter is $COUNTER
            COUNTER=COUNTER-1
    done
exit 0
```

This next example is subtly different: it will continue **until** the counter (starting this time at 20) falls below 10:

```
#!/bin/bash
#example of until loop:
 COUNTER=20
        until [  $COUNTER -lt 10 ]; do
            echo COUNTER $COUNTER
             let COUNTER=COUNTER-1
        done
exit 0
```

Or, in other words, *while* continues as long as a condition **IS** true, but *until* continues as long as it is **NOT** true.

A loop built with *for* will take all the values returned by a command (ls in this case) and act on them one at a time. In this case, each line of output from ls will be read in the i variable and then printed by echo. When the last line has been printed, the loop will stop.

This, by the way, is an example of command substitution: where the ls command is inserted into the for loop to generate input. Command substitution can sound terribly complicated, but it's really nothing more than reassigning a command's output:

```
#!/bin/bash
#example of for loop:
        for i in $( ls ); do
            echo item: $i
        done
exit 0
```

The *for* tool can take input from seq (for sequence), which itself produces numbers in sequence. Before creating a script, let's try out seq on the command line, giving it a numeric value:

```
seq 10
```

As you can see for yourself, seq will count from 1 to 10. Big deal. So can I. Okay, but it can also be told where to start:

```
seq 5 15
```

Yawn.

How about this: you can tell it to count in specified increments (this will count up from 4 to 34 in increments of 6):

```
seq 4 6 34
```

I'll assume that you're still not particularly impressed. However, turning this tool loose in a scripting environment, where it can be used to keep track of time or outside events, might actually prove useful. Here's a very simple example:

```
#!/bin/bash
for i in `seq 15`
  do
      echo "The current number in the sequence is $i."
  done
exit 0
```

Finally, you might sometimes need to launch Linux shell commands from within programs written in other languages like C, Perl, or PHP. This can often be done by simply prefacing the command with *exec*. Here's an example in PHP:

```
exec("dir", $output, $return);
```

SQL Data Management

The LPI doesn't expect you to be a database guru, but you really do need at least a basic idea of how relational databases (SQL) work and of how they can be installed and integrated into a server operation.

The LPIC exam focuses on the SQL command set, which has until recently been most widely used by the open source MySQL engine. This has been complicated by the recent MariaDB fork of the MySQL project and by the success of Amazon Aurora for their RDS (Relational Database Service). But, from your perspective right now, this needn't worry you, because all three of those engines will use the same functionality and even command base.

For this guide, let's imagine an online company that requires a database to track and manage business communications.

You will need to create a table, called contacts, in which each record will represent all the data associated with a single e-mail message. As you can see illustrated in Figure 5-1, each record will be made up of fields for the date/time, the customer's e-mail address, the text of the message, and any follow-up responses.

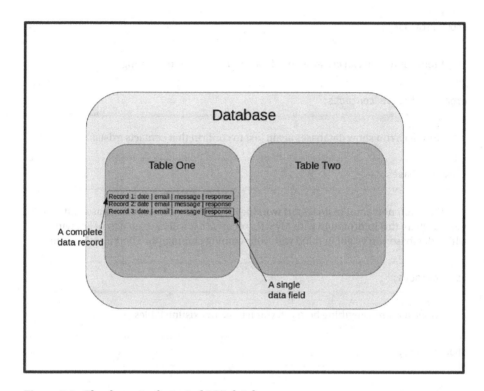

Figure 5-1. *The elements of a typical SQL database*

First, you'll need to install the database. Let's go with MySQL:

```
sudo apt-get update
sudo apt-get install mysql-server
```

You will be asked for a root database password during the installation process. Try not to forget it. Once everything is installed, you can log in as root to the MySQL shell:

```
mysql -u root -p
```

Typing -u introduces the username and -p gets the shell to prompt you for your password. You will now be inside the SQL shell.

One important detail: every command must be followed by a semicolon (;). If it's not, SQL will move to a new line but do nothing. This can be confusing and frustrating, but the shell is just waiting for you to wake up and finish what you were saying (i.e., type the ;).

You can list all current databases using:

```
show databases;
```

Predictably, you can create a new database named contacts using:

```
create database contacts;
```

Now, let's run show databases again just to confirm that contacts exists:

```
show databases;
```

What you now want to do is start working on your new contacts database. But you'll need to share this information with MySQL, otherwise it will have no way of knowing which database you've got in mind with your coming commands. Therefore, let's run:

```
use contacts;
```

To see if there's anything here yet, you'll look for existing tables:

```
show tables;
```

Nothing.

So let's create a new table called emails that will contain records called date, email, message, and response. Each string that is designated as VARCHAR (a variable length character string) must be given a maximum length:

```
create table emails (date DATE, email VARCHAR(20),
message VARCHAR(250), response VARCHAR(250));
```

Now you can manually insert a few records' worth of data. This isn't the way things would normally work. It's far more common to create a program using, say, PHP, that accepts data via user input or some programmatic operations. But, under the hood, this is the format all such actions will use:

```
insert into emails (date,email,message,response) values
('2016-09-12','stan@angry.com','Where's my shipment?',
'Which shipment?');
```

Notice how you first identify all the fields for which you have data (date,email,message,response), and then enter the content itself, separated by apostrophes and commas. Syntax counts!

For practice, perhaps you should add two or three more records following this pattern.

Once you've got some data happily settling into its new home, you will probably want to see it. You can view your data (or, more commonly, "call it" for some kind of processing) using *select*:

```
select * from emails;
```

This example will select all asterisked (*) records from the emails table.

You can also insert data into specified fields by declaring only those you plan to populate. In this example, you have nothing to insert into the response field:

```
insert into emails (date,email,message) values
('2016-09-12','jeff@yahoo.com','hello');
```

This command will select all the contents of every record whose e-mail is equal to stan@angry.com:

```
select * from emails where email='stan@angry.com';
```

This next example will delete those same contents. In fact, it can be very useful to use select as a dry run before deleting anything to confirm that this formulation will deliver exactly what you want:

```
delete * from emails where email='stan@angry.com';
```

You can globally search and replace the contents of specific fields using *update*. This next example will update the e-mail address field from stan@angry.com to stanley@angry.com:

```
update complaints
set email='stanley@angry.com', message='I quit'
where email='stan@angry.com';
```

By the way, if you don't specify "where email=", MySQL will assume that you want to populate every e-mail and message field across the entire table with this new data. You might also note that, this time, you spread the single command across multiple lines by simply leaving the semicolon until the very end.

You can control the order by which records are displayed using order by while DESC tells MySQL to display in descending order:

```
select * from emails order by Date;
select * from emails order by Date DESC;
```

Where order by will change the order by which records are displayed, group by allows you to list multiple records that share some common field in a single line, along with a computed total value.

■ **Note** The following example is borrowed from the excellent SQL tutorial at http://www.w3schools.com/sql/sql_groupby.asp. With their examples and sandbox "try it yourself" pages, w3schools is a great place to learn web development skills.

Let's imagine a database containing two tables: Shippers and Orders. The Shippers table includes a field called ShipperName. The Orders table includes a field called ShipperID, which identifies the shipper associated with each order, and another field called OrderID. You'd like to display the total number of orders placed using each of the three shippers in this system. To do that, you'll have to select data from each of the tables, join it together, and group by (or, in other words, count) all the orders sent through each shipper. Here's how it's done:

```
SELECT    Shippers.ShipperName,COUNT(Orders.OrderID)    AS NumberOfOrders
FROM Orders
LEFT JOIN Shippers
ON Orders.ShipperID=Shippers.ShipperID
GROUP BY ShipperName;
```

Now Try This

Write a script that asks for a user's telephone area code and test to see if he lives within a hundred miles or so from you.

Extra points if you can do the same thing after asking for the user's complete phone number (i.e., if you can figure out how to extract the area code digits from the longer number).

Test Yourself

1. The first file read for a new login session is:

    a. /etc/bash.bashrc

    b. /etc/profile

    c. ~/.bashrc

    d. ~/.bash_login

2. The first line of a shell script must include:

    a. !#/bin/bash

    b. #!/lib/bash

    c. #!/bin/bash

    d. !#/var/bash

3. The script command that will accept user input is:

    a. read

    b. input

    c. echo -r

    d. declare

4. Which of these will continue as long as COUNTER is higher than 9?

    a. while [$COUNTER -lt 10]; do

    b. until [$COUNTER -lt 9]; do

    c. while [$COUNTER -lt 11]; do

    d. until [$COUNTER -lt 10]; do

5. Which of the following is correct?

    a. insert into emails (date,email,message,response) values ('2016- 09-12','jeff@yahoo.com','hello');

    b. insert into emails (date,email,message) values ('2016-09-12','jeff@yahoo.com','hello');

    c. insert into emails (date,email,message) values ('2016-09-12''jeff@yahoo.com''hello');

    d. insert into emails (date,email,message) values ('2016-09-12','jeff@yahoo.com','hello')

6. Which of these will accomplish your exact goals?

    a. set email='stanley@angry.com', message='I quit' where email='stan@angry.com';

    b. set email='stanley@angry.com', message='I quit';

    c. set email='stanley@angry.com' message='I quit' where email='stan@angry.com';

    d. get email='stanley@angry.com', message='I quit' where email='stan@angry.com';

Answer Key

1. b, 2. c, 3. a, 4. d, 5. b, 6. a

■ ■ ■

## CHAPTER 6

Topic 106: User Interfaces and Desktops

If you can read (and if you've made it this far into the book, the odds are that you can), then you've probably already noticed my distinct preference for use of the command line. Nevertheless, there's a reason even Linux offers such a rich choice of graphic user interface (GUI) tools and environments. Just try logging into Netflix from the command line using curl and you'll understand what I mean. So setting up and managing GUI desktops is definitely going to be an important part of a Linux admin's job.

I can tell you that, when it comes to handling graphic devices, Linux has come a very long way over just the past decade. Not too long ago, adding a new video card or even a mouse was not guaranteed to be a stress-free experience. Even supported devices often required manual edits to arcane and hard-to-find configuration files. At this point, things have improved so much that you might realistically go an entire career without ever having to worry about getting mainstream hardware peripherals up and running.

Nevertheless, because you might also need to work with older systems or with nonstandard, cutting-edge hardware, it is still important to have at least a basic understanding of how things work under the hood.

Install and Configure X11

Let's start with the engine, known as X, that drives the Linux graphic interface. I should provide just a bit of background. X is essentially a server that listens for connections from clients using the X protocol and, when necessary, responds. X11 is an important version of the X protocol and is the one I'll discuss in this chapter.

Once upon a time, X was controlled by settings in the xorg.conf configuration file (or, on some systems, xf86Config). These days, if you look in the /etc/X11/ directory where the xorg.conf configuration file is supposed to live, and odds are that you won't find anything. In fact, since integrating hardware peripherals on Linux has been so successfully automated in recent years, the xorg.conf file is seldom used. Nevertheless, should the need arise, you can create one yourself, and the LPI expects you to know how to do it.

© David Clinton 2016
D. Clinton, *Practical LPIC-1 Linux Certification Study Guide*,
DOI 10.1007/978-1-4842-2358-1_6

Here's what a working xorg.conf file might look like:

```
Section "InputDevice"
    # generated from default
    Identifier      "Mouse0"
    Driver          "mouse"
    Option          "Protocol" "auto"
    Option          "Device" "/dev/psaux"
    Option          "Emulate3Buttons" "no"
    Option          "ZAxisMapping" "4 5"
EndSection

Section "InputDevice"
    # generated from default
    Identifier      "Keyboard0"
    Driver          "kbd"
EndSection

Section "Monitor"
    Identifier      "Monitor0"
    VendorName      "Unknown"
    ModelName       "Unknown"
    HorizSync       28.0 - 33.0
    VertRefresh     43.0 - 72.0
    Option          "DPMS"
EndSection

Section "Device"
    Identifier      "Device0"
    Driver          "nvidia"
    VendorName      "NVIDIA Corporation" EndSection

Section "Screen"
    Identifier      "Screen0"
    Device          "Device0"
    Monitor         "Monitor0"
    DefaultDepth    24
    SubSection      "Display"
        Depth       24
    EndSubSection
EndSection

Section "ServerLayout"
    Identifier      "Layout0"
    Screen      0   "Screen0"
    InputDevice     "Keyboard0" "CoreKeyboard"
    InputDevice     "Mouse0" "CorePointer"
EndSection
```

Let's take a section-by-section look. I begin with two sections called InputDevice—one describing a keyboard and the other a mouse. Since they are each the first device of their kind attached to the system, they are identified, respectively, as Keyboard0 and Mouse0. Their drivers and other configuration data are described in subsequent lines.

The Monitor section similarly sets the hardware profile for the attached monitor, as does the Device section for the video adapter.

The Screen section works a bit differently. Since the monitor and video adapter must obviously work together, Screen binds the two profiles into one unit. The ServerLayout section then binds all hardware profiles (screen, mouse, and keyboard) into a single profile, producing an integrated interface.

If you need help creating your own configuration file, you can find some templates in the /usr/share/X11/xorg.conf.d/ directory. It's also worth mentioning that you can find all kinds of documentation and templates for hundreds of installed programs within the /usr/share/ directory tree.

You should be aware of some excellent resources that allow you to research hardware compatibility before you actually start adding components to a system. Some time back, I was very surprised to discover that checking out video adapters didn't even require that I leave my beloved shell session: the built-in system manuals (man) actually contain a remarkable amount of useful information. Running:

```
man ati
```

for instance—to see which ATI adapters are supported—will open a page that points me to separate pages for Radeon, Rage 128, and Mach64 cards. Opening those pages:

```
man Radeon
```

will provide information on dozens of specific models.

If that doesn't cover the information you're after, you can visit the drivers page of the X.Org Foundation web site for a more complete list:

```
http://www.x.org/wiki/Projects/Drivers/
```

If you want to view your current X settings, run xdpyinfo:

```
xdpyinfo | less
```

Since the command will normally output a significant amount of data, you might want to pipe it to *less* so you can view it one screen at a time.

Running xwininfo will prompt you to click inside any open window on your desktop and then display information on that window:

```
xwininfo
```

And if you need to know more about a particular monitor that's attached to your system (or to a remote system with which you're trying to establish a GUI connection, for that matter), you can view the $DISPLAY variable:

```
echo $DISPLAY
```

This can be especially useful for systems with multiple monitors. I will now ask you to read the following words: X Font server.

I'm sure you can guess what the purpose of the X Font server might once have been, but I will assure you that it has not been used for many, many years and will never be used again. So why do I bring it up at all? Because the LPI expects you to be "familiar" with it. Well, now you are.

Set Up a Display Manager

One thing you will find on all Linux GUI systems is a display manager. A display manager is needed to present a login screen and, once you're logged in, to launch a desktop environment. The X11 protocol will then, on behalf of your environment, manage desktop objects, window control elements, frames, virtual and remote displays, and environment settings.

But right now we're only interested in display managers. And, in particular, the new LightDM manager (whose login screen is shown in Figure 6-1). Its relatively small set of tasks is what makes it so fast and, presumably, is what gives it its name ("light").

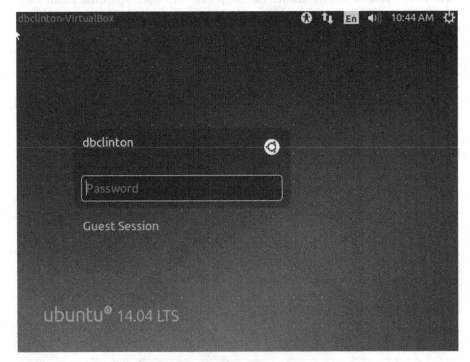

Figure 6-1. The familiar LightDM login screen on Ubuntu 14.04

90

Since LightDM is the manager that currently gets the most attention from the LPI, that will be your main focus. While LightDM stores its main configuration settings within files in the /usr/share/lightdm/lightdm.conf.d/ directory, you can override those settings by editing (or creating) files in /etc/lightdm/lightdm.conf.d/ and the /etc/lightdm/ lightdm.conf file. LightDM, when it loads, will read all of those files in that order. Here are the contents of my /etc/lightdm/lightdm.conf file:

```
[SeatDefaults]
user-session=gnome-fallback
```

The file's only entry tells you that my desktop is set to Gnome-Fallback (as opposed to another desktop like Unity, KDE, or Gnome). Here's the 50-guest-wrapper.conf file from the /usr/share/lightdm/lightdm.conf.d directory:

```
[SeatDefaults]
guest-wrapper=/usr/lib/lightdm/lightdm-guest-session
```

You can see that these files can be very simple. There are, however, a number of optional entries you can add. If you want only users with accounts to be able to log in, and don't want to allow guests, add an allow-guest line and set it accordingly:

```
allow-guest=false
```

You can force all users to be guests, so that any files or settings they create will be erased at the end of their sessions. This can be useful if you're providing a public kiosk and you don't want users to have any permanent system rights:

```
autologin-guest=true
```

If you would prefer that your login screen display a pull-down menu listing all existing users, add this:

```
greeter-hide-users=true
```

If you're the only one using your computer, you might like to set the autologin feature (assuming your user name is Steve):

```
autologin-user=steve
```

This next setting will allow you ten seconds to switch to another user before being automatically logged into the account specified by autologin-user=:

```
autologin-user-timeout=10
```

If you want to override the default greeter, add a .desktop file to the /usr/share/ xgreeters/ directory and point to it from the greeter-session line:

```
greeter-session=unity-greeter.desktop
```

Finally, you can have specific commands run on set events by adding them to any of these script lines:

```
display-setup-script=command
display-stopped-script=command
greeter-setup-script=command
session-setup-script=command
session-cleanup-script=command
session-wrapper=command
greeter-wrapper=command
```

Besides LightDM, other common display managers include KDM, GDM (Gnome), and the really old and deprecated XDM. Since I did briefly mention desktops, I should clarify that display managers like LightDM manage the log in, but then pass most control on to whichever of the dozens of available desktop environments a user has installed and selected. Assuming you've installed alternate desktop environments, you can change your default desktop by clicking the edit icon that's usually somewhere near the password field, and selecting the desktop you prefer (see Figure 6-2).

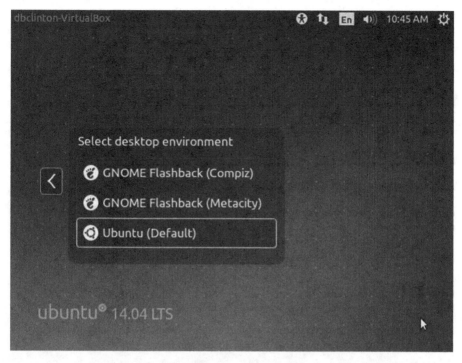

Figure 6-2. Selecting a desktop through the pull-down menu on the login page

Besides your ability to control who can log in to your computer, you can also limit the kinds of remote X sessions that can be started. The tool that does this job is xhost. Typing xhost and the plus sign (+) character will allow anyone to log in to your account from anywhere:

```
xhost +
```

Of course, they'll need to have your password and some way to get past your router and firewall, but this might still be a bit too wide open for normal day-to-day operations. You can, therefore, close access to everyone using:

```
xhost -
```

In case that's too restrictive for your needs, you can permit log ins from individual hosts by entering the source IP address:

```
xhost + 10.0.1.43
```

If an individual source is no longer trusted—or simply no longer needed—you can remove its permission this way:

```
xhost - 10.0.1.43
```

A much more secure and reliable method for allowing remote graphic sessions involves running X11 over SSH, which is something I'll discuss in Chapter 10 (Linux security).

Accessibility

As a Linux administrator, your job will sometimes include providing special assistance to users whose disabilities make working with normal keyboards, mice, and screens difficult. Linux, like all major operating systems, provides a significant set of access tools to help the disabled.

For users with limited or no vision, the brltty daemon provides an interface to many third-party braille display devices, allowing them to read a Linux console:

```
sudo apt-get install brltty
```

While brltty won't work with most graphic screen objects, it can read and interpret text elements. Here is where you will find full documentation:

```
http://mielke.cc/brltty/doc/X11.html
```

Most accessibility tools can be controlled through what Ubuntu calls the Universal Access panel (see Figure 6-3).

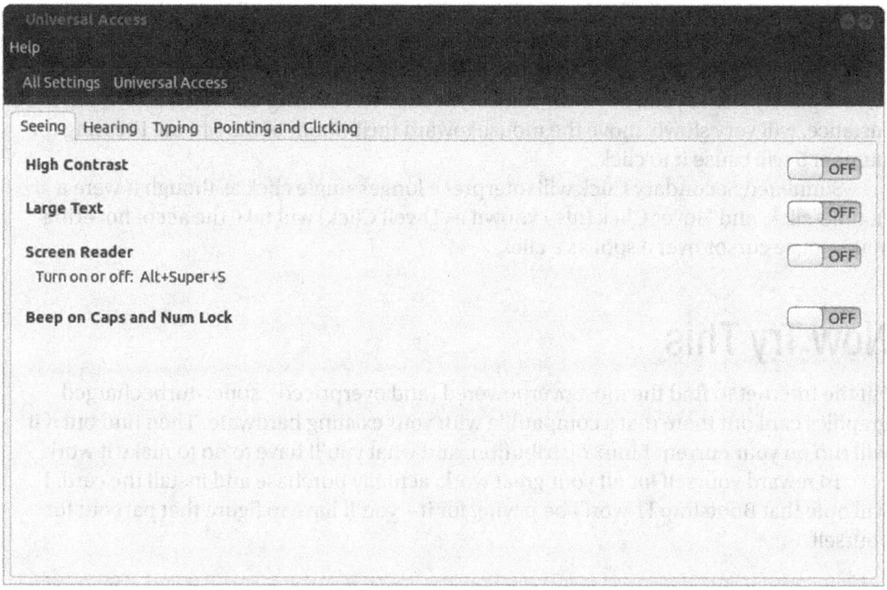

Figure 6-3. *Accessibility for users with various impairments can be managed through the Universal Access panel*

Other distributions might use a slightly different name or appearance, but the tools will all be pretty much the same.

With Screen Reader enabled, a voice will audibly read the screen element that currently has focus. You can also use the Alt+Super+S keystroke combination to enable or disable the reader ("Super," by the way, refers to the Windows Super Key at the bottom left corner of most keyboards). There is more than one screen reading package available, with each offering a different combination of features. Orca and Emacspeak are prominent examples.

High Contrast will convert the desktop theme to colors that are much easier for vision-impaired users to recognize. Large Text will magnify parts of the screen, or at least it should. Unfortunately, the Large Text tool on some Linux distributions appears to be broken right now. You can, however, download KMag that, when you click the *Mouse* button, will follow your mouse around the screen, providing a customizable magnified view.

For people with difficulty using a keyboard or mouse, Linux provides helpful settings. From the Typing tab of Ubuntu's Universal Access panel, you can enable "On Screen Keyboard" (also known as Gnome Onscreen Keyboard, or GOK), which will display a window with a keyboard on which you can type using your mouse. Sticky Keys considers a sequence of keystrokes as though they were typed at the same time. This can be helpful for people finding it difficult to hold down, say, the Alt and Tab keys together. Sticky Keys can be toggled on and off from the Universal Access panel, or by typing the Shift key five times in a row.

Slow Keys increases the time between a key being pressed and the time it is recorded. Since keys must be held for longer before they "count," people who have trouble hitting the right keys the first time will find the process easier.

To avoid accidentally duplicated keystrokes, Bounce Keys will ignore keystrokes that come too quickly after a previous key is pressed.

When Mouse Keys is enabled (from the Pointing and Clicking tab of the Universal Access panel), the keypad keys will control the mouse. Pressing the down arrow, for instance, will very slowly move the mouse toward the bottom of the screen. Pressing the number 5 will cause it to click.

Simulated Secondary Click will interpret a longer single click as though it were a double-click, and Hover Click (also known as Dwell Click) will take the act of hovering your mouse cursor over a spot as a click.

Now Try This

Hit the Internet to find the most overpowered (and overpriced), super-turbocharged graphics card out there that's compatible with your existing hardware. Then find out if it will run on your current Linux distribution, and what you'll have to do to make it work.

To reward yourself for all your great work, actually purchase and install the card. I will note that Bootstrap IT won't be paying for it—you'll have to figure that part out for yourself.

Test Yourself

1. Which section in the xorg.conf file binds all elements together?

    a. Screen

    b. Device

    c. ServerLayout

    d. InputDevice

2. Which section in the xorg.conf file binds the video devices together?

    a. Screen

    b. Monitor

    c. Device

    d. InputDevices

3. Which of the following will display information about your X settings?

    a. xwininfo

    b. man trident

    c. echo $DISPLAY

    d. xdpyinfo

4. Which of the following does NOT contain settings to manage your display manager?

   a. /etc/lightdm/lightdm.conf

   b. /etc/share/lightdm/lightdm.conf.d/

   c. /etc/lightdm/lightdm.conf.d/

   d. /usr/share/lightdm/lightdm.conf.d/

5. Which of these will provide a kiosk environment?

   a. autologin-guest=true

   b. autologin-user-timeout=10

   c. allow-guest=false

   d. session-setup-script=command

6. Which of these will interpret sequential keystrokes as though they occurred at the same time?

   a. Bounce Keys

   b. Mouse Keys

   c. Sticky Keys

   d. Simulated Secondary Click

Answer Key

1. c, 2. a, 3. d, 4. b, 5. a, 6. c

■ ■ ■

## CHAPTER 7

Topic 107: Administrative Tasks

Linux distributions generally work smoothly right out of the box. Still, in the interests of security and reliability, many of the things you'll want to do with your Linux OS will require some fine tuning. So, for instance, resources belonging to certain users might include the kind of sensitive information that needs protection from outside eyes; remote backups and system monitoring tasks need to be automated; and all users, sooner or later, are going to complain about some peculiarities of their spell checkers.

System optimization, therefore, will be the focus of this chapter.

Manage User and Group Accounts

Since Linux was designed as a multiuser environment whose resources can be widely shared, it needs a reliable system for managing access. The structural units that make it all work are user accounts and group accounts. As mentioned previously, every object within a Linux filesystem has a unique set of permissions, dictating who may use it and how. Thus, as long as only the right people are signed in to their accounts and your permissions are all set correctly, you can be sure that everything will work the way it should.

Users

A user's basic profile—including username, UID and GID, home directory, and default shell—is included in the /etc/passwd file. Here's an example showing the user name, group ID, home directory, and shell:

```
steve:x:1013:1013:,,,:/home/steve:/bin/bash
```

Many years ago, an encrypted version of each user's password would also be stored in passwd but, since passwd needs open read permissions, that led to unacceptable vulnerabilities. Instead, encrypted passwords are stored in the /etc/shadow file, which is read by the system whenever a user attempts to log in. If you try to read the shadow file, you will find that you're not allowed unless you invoke admin privileges:

© David Clinton 2016
D. Clinton, *Practical LPIC-1 Linux Certification Study Guide*,
DOI 10.1007/978-1-4842-2358-1_7

```
sudo cat /etc/shadow
```

Here's a sample entry from shadow (with a truncated version of the encrypted password):

```
steve:$6$0YGemJFs$fhLFANy.O4.0:16807:0:99999:7:::
```

For many Linux distributions, user accounts are managed using the useradd, userdel, and usermod tools.

■ **Note**   I should mention that some distributions, including Debian and Ubuntu, prefer adduser and deluser etc., which, with some subtle differences, cover pretty much the same ground. However, since the LPI wants you to focus on useradd, that's what I'll do here.

You can add a new user and, depending on your /etc/login.defs settings, a new group of the same name by simply running useradd followed by the name you'd like for the new account:

```
sudo useradd -m mark
```

The -m tells Linux to create a home directory for the new user, which, by default in this case, will be /home/mark. Unless you specify otherwise, the contents of the /etc/skel directory (known as the skeleton directory) will be copied to the new home directory. By default, useradd will not prompt you to create a new password for the account. You will have to run passwd to manually add one:

```
sudo passwd mark
```

Passwd can also be used to update an existing user's password.

■ **Note**   In case you're wondering, I'm afraid I, too, can't explain why the Unix password command is spelled passwd. Perhaps the author of the program (Julie Haugh) **really** didn't like typing. I guess this will just have to be one of the many mysteries that add spice to our otherwise dull, daily lives.

Adding arguments to useradd can further define account attributes. Table 7-1 provides some examples (see man useradd for more).

Table 7-1. *Examples of Arguments to Define Attributes*

–G (or –groups)	Adds the new user to other groups.
–s (or --shell)	Specifies a default shell for user logins.
–u (or --uid)	Lets you manually specify a UID (rather than the UID that would otherwise be automatically assigned).

You can remove a user from the system using userdel:

```
sudo userdel stanley
```

To edit an account's settings once it already exists, you can run usermod. You can, for instance, set a date on which the account will expire using:

```
sudo usermod -e 2017-12-31 mark
```

You can change Mark's login name to Henry with -l:

```
sudo usermod -l henry mark
```

This will NOT change the account name or the name of his home directory.

If you want to temporarily lock Mark (or Henry, as I guess he's now known) out of his account, you can use:

```
sudo usermod -L henry
```

Using -U will unlock his account and -G will add or remove membership in a group:

```
sudo usermod -G sudo henry
```

Perhaps the greatest security weakness your system will face is its passwords, and the last person you should trust with the creation of a strong and secure password is a human being. Yet, there aren't usually all that many alternatives. Ideally, all our users should use password vault software packages like Figaro or KeePassX, which can generate very strong passwords and make them conveniently available when needed. But even that won't solve a different problem: how to get people to regularly update their passwords.

You can use chage to force users to do just that:

```
sudo chage -m 5 -M 30 Max
```

This will force Max to update his password no less than five days, but no more than 30 days since his previous update (m = minimum, M = maximum). Using:

```
sudo chage -W 7 Max
```

will send Max a warning seven days before his deadline. You can list Max's current settings using:

```
sudo chage --list Max
```

Groups

For all their value, there are limits to the flexibility of an object's permissions. Let's say that you've got a directory containing sensitive documents that you want some, but not all, users to be able to both read and edit. One way to give an individual user those rights is to make him the object's owner, but that would exclude everyone else. Another method is to open up access to all users, but that might be far too permissive for your needs.

The solution is to create a group and give it rights over the directory. You can then add all the users who need rights to the group.

Here's how it works. You create a new group—let's call it backoffice—with:

```
sudo groupadd backoffice
```

Then you can add all the necessary users to the group using usermod -G for each user (as above), or by adding the user names to the backoffice line from the /etc/group file. Just remember to add only a comma (and no space) between each name on the line.

Here's an entry from the /etc/group file showing the sudo (admin) group and its two current members:

```
sudo:x:27:mike,steve
```

Using groupmod will let you change some details, like the group name:

```
sudo groupmod -n frontoffice backoffice
```

And groupdel will—all together now—delete a group:

```
sudo groupdel frontoffice
```

You should be aware that, just as the /etc/passwd file contains information about users, the /etc/group file is a list of all current groups. While I'm on that topic, you can use getent to display the entries of a number of Name Service Switch libraries, including passwd, group, hosts, aliases, and networks:

```
getent passwd
```

Automate System Administration Tasks

It's a sad fact that many of the most important administrative tasks are far more likely to get done if they don't have to rely on you to do them. People forget stuff and get distracted by all kinds of things (most of which are featured on YouTube "You might like ..." panels). So if you want to make absolutely sure that your critical data backups and log-file rotations happen when they should, automate 'em.

Linux offers three main scheduling tools to help you out on this: cron, anacron, and at.

Using cron

The cron system is actually very simple to use. If you list items in the /etc/ directory with cron in their names, you'll get this:

```
$ ls -l /etc/ | grep cron
-rw-r--r--  1 root root     401 Dec 20  2012 anacrontab
drwxr-xr-x  2 root root    4096 Nov 22 22:21 cron.d
drwxr-xr-x  2 root root    4096 Dec 21 12:29 cron.daily
drwxr-xr-x  2 root root    4096 Oct 16  2013 cron.hourly
drwxr-xr-x  2 root root    4096 Apr 27  2014 cron.monthly
-rw-r--r--  1 root root     722 Feb  9  2013 crontab
drwxr-xr-x  2 root root    4096 Nov 22 22:12 cron.weekly
```

Right now, you're interested in the cron.daily, cron.hourly, cron.weekly, and cron. monthly directories. If you want a script to automatically run at any one of those intervals, just save it to the appropriate directory and forget about it (assuming, of course, that you made the script executable using chmod +x). This works because crontab—as directed by the /etc/crontab file—regularly reads and then executes any scripts found in these directories. Here's my system's crontab file:

```
$ cat /etc/crontab
# m h dom mon dow user command
17 * * * * root            cd    /   &&   run-parts   --report
/etc/cron.hourly
25 6 * * * root test -x /usr/sbin/anacron || ( cd / && run- parts --report /
etc/cron.daily )
```

```
47 6 * * 7 root test -x /usr/sbin/anacron || ( cd / && run- parts --report /
etc/cron.weekly )
52 6 1 * * root test -x /usr/sbin/anacron || ( cd / && run- parts --report
/etc/cron.monthly )
```

The commented-out line at the top of the file tells us what each column represents. The first field (17, in the first row) is the number of minutes into an hour at which the scripts will be executed. The second column (h) is the hour of the day; dom stands for day of month, mon for month, and dow for day of week. Which means that the scripts in the first row will be executed 17 minutes after the start of each hour, on each day of every month, regardless of which day of the week it comes out on.

This, of course, makes sense for scripts saved to cron.hourly. To take the last row as another example, scripts in the cron.monthly directory will be executed once on the first day of each month at 6:52 a.m.

By the way, for compatibility reasons, the numbers 0 and 7 of the dow column both refer to Sunday.

Although the file shown above was the general system crontab, each individual user will have their own crontab file. Technically, user crontabs are kept in the /var/spool/cron directory tree, but you shouldn't really work with those. Instead, running:

```
crontab -e
```

will open an editor with excellent documentation where you can create your own cron jobs.

While this isn't on the LPIC exam, you should be aware that crontab functionality can be handled on Systemd distributions using timer units. When you do set up your first Systemd job, you will probably discover that they're a bit more complicated than cron. You'll first need to create a file with the .timer extension in /etc/systemd/system/, then another file with a .target extension in the same directory to act as its target, and finally a third file as a service (with a .service extension). You then activate the job through systemctl:

```
systemctl enable   /etc/systemd/system/jobname.timer
systemctl start    /etc/systemd/system/jobname.timer
systemctl enable   /etc/systemd/system/servicename.service
```

Using anacron

Cron works wonderfully for servers that are running 24 hours a day. However, if you're managing workstations or PCs that are turned off at night and over weekends—or virtualized Docker-like containers that may only live for a few minutes or hours—then you'll need a different solution. Welcome to anacron.

The anacrontab file that's kept in the /etc/ directory looks a bit like crontab, except that there are far fewer columns controlling timing. Here's a sample anacrontab file:

```
$ cat /etc/anacrontab
# These replace cron's entries
1    5    cron.daily run-parts --report /etc/cron.daily
7    10   cron.weekly run-parts --report /etc/cron.weekly
@monthly 15   cron.monthly     run-parts        --report
/etc/cron.monthly
```

The first column sets the number of days you want to leave between executions. The number 1 would execute the job every day, while the number 7 would do it once a week. Populating the field with the value @monthly indicates a single execution each month. The next column tells anacron how long, in minutes, the system should wait after booting before executing the command.

During this discussion of crontab, you will have no doubt noticed that the final three jobs in the crontab file included test -x /usr/sbin/anacron. This will check to see if anacron is executable and, if it is **NOT** available, execute the job that follows.

Using at

The at program allows a command or script to be scheduled for a **single** execution at some later time. The scheduling function is actually quite flexible and can take a number of formats. You can, for instance, schedule an event relative to the current time:

```
at now +15 minutes
```

You could also use one of a number of designations for the next occurrence of an absolute time:

```
at 14:30
at noon
at midnight
at teatime
```

Teatime, by the way, is the break enjoyed at four in the afternoon by many in England (and in some lands under their influence).

You schedule an at job by typing a time as above and, in the new shell that will open, the command or commands you'd like to be executed. When you're done, press Ctrl+d to exit the shell:

```
at 14:30
> cat /etc/passwd > ~/useraccounts.txt
```

You can run atq to display a list of pending at jobs along with their IDs:

```
atq
```

With that information, you can cancel a pending job using atrm:

```
atrm <ID>
```

The *batch* program (even though it shares a name with the old DOS.BAT files) works much the same as using at, but it will only execute a job if the system load levels permit it.

The /var/spool/cron directory contains *cron* and *at* files created by regular users.

Finally, you can control which of your users are allowed to create *at* or *cron* jobs through whitelists and blacklists. If any users appear in the at.allow file in /etc/, then they—and only they—will be permitted to create at jobs. If there is no at.allow file, or if the file is empty, then all users will be permitted to create at jobs except for those listed explicitly in the at.deny file. The exact same protocol is followed for the cron.allow and cron.deny files.

Localization and Internationalization

In an age when just about every device is networked, if you want your machines to be able to reliably talk to each other, maintaining the correct time, time zone, and locale is more important than ever. You can display the system time and date using date. The --set argument lets you set the date and time in this format:

```
date --set="20160625 06:10:00"
```

On Systemd systems, timedatectl acts in much the same way. You can set your system to synchronize with an NTP server using:

```
timedatectl set-ntp true
```

Information on time zones throughout the world is kept in the /usr/share/zoneinfo directory tree. You might have to drill down a level or two to get to your city. The function of these files is to serve as targets to which you can link to obtain time zone data.

You can update your system time zone setting by creating a symbolic link between the /etc/localtime file and the appropriate time zone source file. In my case, it might work like this:

```
ls -sf /usr/share/zoneinfo/America/Toronto /etc/localtime
```

Another way to do the same thing is by running either *tzselect* or *dpkg- reconfigure tzdata* and following instructions. Just in case three alternative tools aren't enough for you, you can also update your time zone by manually editing the /etc/timezone file, creating a TZ system variable using:

```
export TZ=Asia/Manila
```

or, on Systemd systems (and assuming you live in New York), through:

```
sudo timedatectl set-timezone America/New_York
```

I believe that this is the most overserved system setting in all of Linuxdom.

You can, by the way, add Systemd functionalityto non-systemd systems by installing the systemd-services package:

```
sudo apt-get install systemd-services
```

Besides your time and time zone settings, you also have to worry about locale. But what, you might ask, is locale?

Besides languages and alphabets, the way you represent certain values will differ depending on where you live. Even among English-speaking countries, for instance, there are significant variations in spelling. There are, as another example, quite a few formats used to write dates using numbers. (For the life of me, I can never remember whether I'm supposed to understand 15/04/06 as June 4, 2015, March 6, 2015, or March 15, 2004.)

These values are all controlled by the localization settings. To list your current locale settings, run:

```
$ locale
LANG=en_CA.UTF-8
LANGUAGE=
LC_CTYPE="en_CA.UTF-8"
LC_NUMERIC=en_CA.UTF-8
LC_TIME=en_CA.UTF-8
LC_COLLATE="en_CA.UTF-8"
LC_MONETARY=en_CA.UTF-8
LC_MESSAGES="en_CA.UTF-8"
LC_PAPER=en_CA.UTF-8
LC_NAME=en_CA.UTF-8
LC_ADDRESS=en_CA.UTF-8
LC_TELEPHONE=en_CA.UTF-8
LC_MEASUREMENT=en_CA.UTF-8
LC_IDENTIFICATION=en_CA.UTF-8
LC_ALL=
```

As you can see, there's quite a list of locale categories. They can each be set separately but, by default, they all follow the LANG setting.

Before you can change your locale, you'll need to know which alternate locales are available to you. To list them, run:

```
locale -a
```

To list all *supported* locales (even those that aren't currently locally available), view the /usr/share/i18n/SUPPORTED file:

```
cat /usr/share/i18n/SUPPORTED
```

To import a supported locale, run locale-gen. This example will make the Russia locale, using UTF-8 encoding, available:

```
locale-gen ru_RU.UTF-8
```

Then, running:

```
LANG=ru_RU.utf8
```

will set that locale, but only for the current shell session. Adding export LANG=en_US.utf8 to the ~/.bashrc or ~/.profile file will make that locale permanent for that user. You will need to log out and log in again for the change to take effect.

Changing the LANG variable in the /etc/default/locale file to read like this:

```
LANG="en_US.utf8"
```

which will set the locale for **all** users. Again, this will only take effect for new sessions.

Table 7-2 lists some of those locale categories and their purposes.

Table 7-2. *Some Common Linux Locale Values*

LC_TIME	Date and time formats.
LC_NUMERIC	Nonmonetary numeric formats.
LC_MONETARY	Monetary formats.
LC_PAPER	Paper size (i.e., A4 for Europe and Letter for North America).
LC_ADDRESS	Address formats and location information.
LC_TELEPHONE	Telephone number formats.
LC_MEASUREMENT	Measurement units (Metric or Other).
LC_IDENTIFICATION	Metadata about the locale information.

LC_ALL= will, when given a value, apply that value to all locale categories.

LANG=C is another special locale setting that can sometimes be useful. This will emulate C language syntax and conventions and is used because it's very unlikely to cause conflicts, given that C is the programming language in which most operating systems were written.

Finally, character encoding can play a large role in localization. The example I used above specified UTF-8 as the default encoding, and that's generally a very safe bet. However, there are other options, including ISO-8859, ASCII, and Unicode.

Should you need it, you can use the iconv program to convert a text file between character encodings:

```
iconv -f ascii -t utf8 oldfilename > newfilename
```

Now Try This

Create a new directory called /var/opt/myapp to store program data from your (imaginary) myapp application. Next, create a new group called myapp and give it rights over the directory. Finally, create a new user and add him to the myapps group, but *do not* give the new user sudo rights.

Switch to the new user using su and try to copy a file to the /var/opt/myapp directory to confirm that everything is working the way it should.

Test Yourself

1. Encrypted passwords are stored in which of these?

    a. /etc/passwd

    b. /etc/usermod

    c. /usr/passwd

    d. /etc/shadow

2. Which of these will suspend a user's account?

    a. sudo usermod -L henry

    b. sudo usermod -l henry

    c. sudo usermod -s henry

    d. sudo usermod -G henry

3. Which of these will set a maximum expiry date for a user's password?

    a. sudo chage -m 30 Max

    b. sudo chage -M 30 Max

    c. sudo passwd -m 30 Max

    d. sudo shadow -M 30 Max

4. How can you change a group name from backoffice to frontoffice?

   a. sudo groupmod -n backoffice frontoffice

   b. sudo groupmod -n frontoffice backoffice

   c. sudo groupadd -n backoffice frontoffice

   d. sudo groupadd -w backoffice frontoffice

5. When will this crontab job execute?: 30 14 * * 3

   a. 2:00 p.m. every day of March.

   b. 2:30 p.m. every Wednesday of every month.

   c. 2:30 a.m. every Tuesday of every month.

   d. 2:30 p.m. every Monday of every month.

6. When will this anacron job execute?: 7 20

   a. Once a week, at least 20 minutes after boot and assuming there is no overlapping crontab job.

   b. Once a week assuming it's after the 20th of the month.

   c. Once a week, at least 20 minutes after boot.

   d. On the 20th of the month, seven minutes after boot.

7. To prevent all users besides Henry from creating at jobs, create ____:

   a. an at.allow file with his name in it.

   b. an at.deny file with his name in it.

   c. an at.deny file with the names of all other users in it.

   d. a cron.allow file with his name in it.

8. Which of these will NOT work to update your time zone?

   a. ls -sf /usr/share/zoneinfo/America/Toronto /etc/localtime

   b. export TZ=Asia/Manila

   c. dpkg-reconfigure tzselect

   d. sudo timedatectl set-timezone America/New_York

Answer Key

1. d, 2. a, 3. b, 4. b, 5. b, 6. c, 7. a, 8. c

■ ■ ■

## CHAPTER 8

Topic 108: Essential System Services

Like all operating systems, Linux quietly provides a number of seemingly minor, but critical, services. In this chapter, you'll learn about managing the Linux services that oversee the accuracy of your time settings, the way events are logged, and e-mail and printing facilities. These things may not seem all that exciting, but just imagine what life would be like for you as an administrator if any one of them ever failed.

Maintain System Time

Besides ensuring that your computer's time zone setting is correct, as discussed in Chapter 7, it's also critically important to make sure that your system time is in sync with reality. This is true for anyone using a PC or smartphone who doesn't want to arrive late for a dentist appointment, but it's many, many times more true for an application server that's processing financial transactions whose time stamps simply must be completely accurate.

I was once involved in an IT project that required closely coordinating the behavior of dozens of routers to within 1/100 of a second of each other. If I got that wrong, we risked the loss of thousands of dollars of equipment.

So, having said that, have you got the time?

The Hardware Clock

Well, as it turns out, the answer to that question will depend on which part of your computer you're talking to. The hardware clock (also known as the BIOS clock, the CMOS clock, or the real-time clock [RTC]) will respond one way, and the software system time will often respond with something else. That's largely because, when left to its own devices (so to speak), the hardware clock measures time in complete isolation from the rest of the world. Just like the time on your quartz watch will sometimes be a bit behind or ahead, the CMOS battery can lead the hardware clock astray in relation to network time.

© David Clinton 2016
D. Clinton, *Practical LPIC-1 Linux Certification Study Guide*,
DOI 10.1007/978-1-4842-2358-1_8

The system clock, on the other hand, can be synchronized with highly accurate NTP (Network Time Protocol) time servers over the Internet. I'll discuss setting up NTP connectivity in a just a minute or two, but first, let's look at the relationship between the hardware and system clocks.

As already mentioned, you can display the system time through the date command:

```
date
```

You can display the current hardware time with:

```
sudo hwclock -r
```

When everything is said and done, is it really healthy to have two conflicting times being used on one machine? It's not always a problem, as software services tend to work exclusively with the system time, but in those cases where you need to coordinate things, help is at hand. You can update your system clock so it will be set to the current hardware time using hctosys:

```
sudo hwclock --hctosys
```

And you can update your hardware time to match the system value using systohc:

```
sudo hwclock --systohc
```

Once your hardware clock is properly set, you might also want it to report time according to your local time zone or to a different value, usually UTC (Coordinated Universal Time, a common international standard):

```
sudo hwclock --localtime
sudo hwclock --utc
```

You can also manually set the hardware time using this format:

```
hwclock --set --date="8/10/16 13:30:00"
```

Network Time Protocol (NTP)

If you want to properly coordinate your system time with a reliable network time provider, you'll need to use some kind of NTP service. The ntpdate program can be used from the command line or from within a script to update your system time to one or more specified network servers. One variation of this for Debian or Ubuntu systems is ntpdate-debian:

```
sudo ntpdate-debian
```

By default, ntpdate-debian will poll the ntp.ubuntu.com server.

If necessary, ntpdate will adjust your system time gradually, to reduce the risk of conflicts. If the local error is less than 128 milliseconds, ntpdate will use slewing to gradually make the change. If the error is greater than 128 milliseconds, then it will use stepping instead. If your system time is more than 1,024 seconds off—known as insane time—no changes will be made until you manually correct it.

Although ntpdate is not nearly as accurate over the long term as NTP, it can sometimes be useful to prepare your system for NTP.

So let's talk about NTP. The NTP service—effectively the product of the labor of just one man: David L. Mills of the University of Delaware—draws on reliable time sources like the US Naval Observatory in Bethesda, Maryland.

A server that takes its time directly from a primary source like the observatory is called a stratum 1 server. Servers that are configured to receive their time from a stratum 1 server are known as stratum 2 servers, and so on until stratum 15.

Obviously, the closer your computer (known as a consumer) is to stratum 1, the more reliable its time will be. However, if all computers tried to take their time from a single stratum 1 server, the load might become too great to handle. To prevent this, NTP prefers that you set your NTP configuration to get its time from an NTP pool.

Let's see how all this works. You can install the NTP program from the regular repositories. On Debian systems, you can use:

```
sudo apt-get install ntp
```

Once it's installed, you can monitor the service using the ntpq shell, or from the command line by adding parameters to the ntpq command; -p will, for instance, list existing peers:

```
ntpq -p
```

The NTP configuration is kept in the /etc/ntp.conf file. Here are some excerpts from a typical .conf file on an Ubuntu machine. I will describe them as I go along:

```
# /etc/ntp.conf, configuration for ntpd; see ntp.conf(5)
# for help
driftfile /var/lib/ntp/ntp.drift
```

Drift occurs when a clock is either faster or slower than a reference clock (a network time provider, in this case). The drift value, often stored in the ntp.drift file in the /var/lib/ntp/ directory, is measured in parts per million (ppm). If your drift value is a positive number, it means your clock is moving too fast. If it's negative, your clock is slow:

```
# Enable this if you want statistics to be logged.
#statsdir /var/log/ntpstats/
```

The statsdir setting will enable logging of NTP statistics to files in the /var/log/ntpstats/ directory:

```
# Specify one or more NTP servers.
# Use servers from the NTP Pool Project. Approved by
# Ubuntu Technical Board on 2011-02-08 (LP: #104525).
# See http://www.pool.ntp.org/join.html
# for more information.
server 0.ubuntu.pool.ntp.org
server 1.ubuntu.pool.ntp.org
server 2.ubuntu.pool.ntp.org
server 3.ubuntu.pool.ntp.org
```

This is probably the most important section of the file. On Ubuntu systems, servers from the Ubuntu NTP pool are automatically added, sending you randomly to any one of the four. You could, of course, remove these servers and replace them with your own, including private NTP servers within your own network.

The next line designates a fallback server if the pool fails:

```
# Use Ubuntu's ntp server as a fallback.
server ntp.ubuntu.com
```

The last line I'll discuss allows you to set your computer up as a server for other consumers. You would, of course, need to remove the hash symbol (#) from the broadcast line and change the IP address to match the broadcast address of your subnet:

```
# If you want to provide time to your local subnet,
# change the next line.
# (Again, the address is an example only.)
#broadcast 192.168.123.255
```

System Logging

All kinds of Linux services and programs output log data as part of their activities. Whether they're error messages, success notifications, user login records, or system crash information, these messages need to be directed and saved in a way that will make them useful. A common protocol for managing log files and the way they're populated is rsyslog.

Using syslogd

The rsyslog is just one of many syslog log management protocols that allows you to control the creation and movement of log data; rsyslog itself replaced syslog on many systems and seems more widely used. Besides those two, syslog-ng (known for its content-based filtering) and klogd (which focuses on kernel messaging) have also enjoyed widespread adoption.

As you've already seen a number of times, most Linux log files—at least those in traditional Linux architectures—live in or below the /var/log/ directory. On systems using rsyslog, the flow of log data is controlled through the /etc/rsyslog.conf file, which points to additional config files in the /etc/rsyslog.d/ directory. Here is a section from a typical /etc/rsyslog.d/50-default.conf file:

auth,authpriv.*	-/var/log/auth.log
***.*;auth,authpriv.none**	-/var/log/syslog
cron.*	-/var/log/cron.log
daemon.*	-/var/log/daemon.log
kern.*	-/var/log/kern.log
lpr.*	-/var/log/lpr.log
mail.*	-/var/log/mail.log
#user.*	-/var/log/user.log

Let's try to understand what it all means. The information flowing from services can be broken down into a number of facilities:

auth	lpr	security (same as auth)
authpriv	mail	syslog
cron	mark	user
daemon	news	uucp
kern,		

and user-defined facilities are named local0 through local7.

Messages from each of those facilities can be categorized using one of these priority levels:

debug	warn (same as warning)	alert
info	err	emerg
notice	error (same as err)	panic (same as emerg)
warning	crit	

Error, warn, and panic have all been deprecated.

A facility that's represented together with a priority like this:

```
cron.err
```

would be an instruction to log all *error* messages from the *cron* facility to the designated log file (as mentioned in the right-hand column).

With that information, you'll decode the second line of the 50- default.conf file. The *.* means that **all** messages from **all** priority levels will be added to /var/log/syslog, even if they're also sent to other log files. The ;auth,authpriv.none at the end of the facility line means that messages from the auth and authpriv facilities will **NOT** be logged.

You can edit an entry to change its behavior. If you didn't want all mail messages to be added to the mail.log file, you could change mail.* to mail.alert so that only messages of priority alert and higher will be sent, but not those of lower priority.

Using journald

By default, Systemd-based Linux distributions like Red Hat and CentOS (and Ubuntu from 15.04 and up) have replaced individual log files like syslog and dmesg with a single binary logging system managed by journald. The journal itself is written to the /var/log/journal/ directory. You can view and manage logs through *journalctl*. Adding -e, for instance, will display only the 1,000 most recent journal entries from all sources:

```
journalctl -e
```

You can also use journalctl to check how much disk space your logs are currently using. This is more important than you might think, as logs can sometimes grow to enormous sizes and, if left untended, effectively cripple entire systems:

```
$ journalctl --disk-usage
Journals take up 88.0M on disk.
```

You can edit journald settings through the journald.conf file:

```
nano /etc/systemd/journald.conf
```

There, you will be able to set system values like how large the journal file will be allowed to grow (#SystemMaxFileSize=).

Using logger

On first glance, you might think the logger tool is just about as useful as a remote control for a car radio. Now don't laugh: I once had to buy an after-market radio/CD player for my car and it came with a remote. None of the techs who installed it could figure out what it was for either. I mean, just how far could you get from the dashboard while you're driving?

But logger, a tool that lets you post text strings to a log file directly from the command line, might seem just as silly. That is, until you realize that you might sometimes need important events recorded manually with the accurate time stamp of a log file. Or, alternatively, you might want to include a simple logging mechanism within a script. In any case, you should be familiar with logger.

Open up two terminals side by side. In the first, use tail to print ongoing entries in syslog:

```
tail -f /var/log/syslog
```

In the second terminal, type:

```
logger Hello there!
```

You should be able to see your latest "Hello there!" added to the syslog file, along with your account name (the source) and the time/date stamp. You can also control where a message is logged by adding a value for -p:

```
logger -p lpr.crit Help!
```

This will log the word "Help!" to the lpr (printer) log file and categorize it with a priority of crit.

Using logrotate

As mentioned earlier, the sheer volume of log messages produced by a busy Linux system can quickly overwhelm available storage space. Rather than simply deleting files when they grow too large (which can lead to the premature loss of valuable data), the solution is to rotate them. Rotation behavior is controlled by settings in the /etc/logrotate.conf file. Let's look at a few lines from the file.

```
# rotate log files weekly
weekly
```

This sets the system default for log rotation frequency:

```
# keep 4 weeks worth of backlogs
rotate 4
```

This tells the system how long older, rotated logs should be kept before being deleted:

```
# uncomment this if you want your log files compressed
#compress
```

When activated, this setting will compress rotated log files in order to save space:

```
# packages drop log rotation information into this directory include /etc/
logrotate.d
```

This line points to files in the /etc/logrotate.d/ directory where nonsystem packages can keep their own log file rotation config files:

Here's a snippet from the /etc/logrotate.d/apt file that controls rotation rules for logs generated by the apt package manager:

```
/var/log/apt/history.log {
  rotate 12
  monthly
  compress
  missingok
  notifempty
}
```

Mail Transfer Agent Basics

E-mail, despite many earnest predictions to the contrary over the past 20 years or so, is still very much alive and well. And despite the existence of powerful enterprise e-mail solutions from providers like Google, you might still one day be called upon to create an e-mail server to handle mail for a private domain. Having done this myself more than once, I can tell you that it's not nearly as hard as it might seem.

A mail transfer agent (MTA) uses protocols like the Simple Mail Transfer Protocol (SMTP) for sending mail, and the Post Office Protocol 3 (POP3) or Internet Message Access Protocol (IMAP) for receiving.

From the perspective of a command-line user, the four better-known Linux e-mail agents (qmail, postfix, sendmail, and exim) share a similar interface. The truth is, that qmail is no longer maintained, and exim seems to be largely unused, partly due to its poor reputation for security. But the LPI expects you to be at least familiar with their existence.

Here I'll focus on postfix, although most of the commands you will see should work for any package. You prepare your server by installing postfix and mailutils:

```
apt-get install postfix mailutils
```

You'll be asked to set your domain during the installation process, but you can always leave it for now and add it later by editing the mydestination line of the /etc/postfix/main.cf file. You will have to open up port 25 for incoming traffic in order to receive e-mail.

Now that it's installed, you can send mail to a local address (any user account on the system) using the sendmail command:

```
sendmail -t tony
```

You might be prompted for a subject, which you can fill in, and then hit Enter. On the next line, you can compose your message, hitting Enter and then Ctrl+d to save and send the mail.

Typing simply mail at the command line will list all the e-mails your account has received. By typing the number next to a message, you can read it. Typing d after reading it will delete the message, and q will exit the shell. If you have trouble either sending or receiving mail, be sure to check the logs, which, on Debian systems, can be found in the /var/log/mail file.

You can create aliases, which are groups of mail recipients, by editing the /etc/aliases file:

```
sudo nano /etc/aliases
```

Just add a new line with the name of your alias group, a colon, a space, or tab, and the names of the people you want to include:

```
marketing: tony, salesguys@gmail.com, steve@mycompanyname.com
```

To tell postfix about the new alias, run:

```
sudo newaliases
```

and you're done.

Assuming that you chose marketing as the name for your new alias, you can now use the alias name on your e-mail like this:

```
sendmail -t marketing
```

Your e-mail will automatically be sent to all the users listed as part of the alias.

If you would like to forward e-mails received by a particular e-mail account to a different address, create a new file in the home directory of the account whose mail you want forwarded:

```
touch ~/.forward
```

Then add the address to which you want mail forwarded to the file.

```
echo salesguys@gmail.com >> .forward
```

Finally, as you might expect, you can view pending e-mails using mailq:

```
mailq
```

Manage Printers and Printing

Remember that paperless office we were told digital networks and computers would give the world? That one didn't seem to work out so well, did it? Printers today go through more paper than would have ever been possible in the good old days of pencils and desks.

Which is just a way of saying that managing printers is going to be as important a part of any admin's job as it ever was in the past. The only difference is that the quality and reliability of printers have improved. Not to mention that there are now good Linux software drivers available for just about every modern model.

Linux distributions will usually use CUPS (the Common Unix Printing System) to manage printers. You can certainly configure and manage CUPS through the CUPS configuration file at /etc/cups/cupsd.conf, but, as you can see from Figure 8-1, most people access the browser-based interface at http://localhost:631.

Figure 8-1. *The CUPS (Common Unix Printing System) browser administration interface*

Either way, you can use CUPS to perform administrative tasks like adding or removing printers, controlling network accessibility, updating drivers, or managing classes (groups of printers that can be used on an as-available basis). CUPS logs are (on Debian systems at least) usually kept in /var/log/cups, but you can view them in the browser interface as well.

■ **Note**   Fun fact: I'll bet you didn't know that CUPS is feely provided and maintained by Apple. That's right: Apple Inc.

Before there was CUPS, Linux folk printed using the lpd command-line interface. To your unending joy, lpd still exists, and the LPI expects you to be familiar with its workings for their exam. The truth is, though, that the basic lpd commands aren't complicated at all and generally follow the same patterns that we've seen in a number of other places. So don't worry too much about this.

The lp daemon is actually now aware of the CUPS configuration and will therefore know all about your installed printers without requiring your input. If you've never had to manually configure a dot matrix printer connected through a 25-pin parallel cable, you can't really appreciate what good news this is.

Getting started is as simple as pointing to a file:

```
lp mytext.txt
```

If you've got more than one printer connected to your system (or perhaps via a network), you can specify the one you want. This command will print to my Brother laser printer:

```
lp -d DCP7060D mytext.txt
```

If you're not sure what your printer is called, run:

```
lpq
```

You can also print a text stream directly from the command line:

```
echo hello | lp
```

but that just wastes a perfectly fine sheet of paper!

Using lpq will also list any pending print jobs. If you'd like to remove a job (perhaps to clear a jam in the queue), use lprm and the job number:

```
lprm 423
```

Using lprm followed by a dash:

```
lprm -
```

121

will remove all the jobs in the queue.

You can block new jobs from reaching a printer using cupsreject:

```
cupsreject DCP7060D
```

and unblock it with:

```
cupsaccept DCP7060D
```

Now Try This

Write a short script that will execute a command (say, to read the contents of /etc/passwd) and then post a message that indicates success to the auth.alert log facility. Test your script to make sure it works, then use the cron system to make sure it runs regularly, once an hour.

Don't forget to cancel the once-an-hour thing when you're done. You should always clean up your toys when you're done playing with them.

Test Yourself

1. What will sudo hwclock --hctosys do?

    a. Update your hardware time to match the system time.

    b. Display the current hardware time.

    c. Tell the clock to report using UTC.

    d. Update your system time to match the hardware time.

2. The value contained in /var/lib/ntp/ntp.drive is measured in: _____

    a. ppm

    b. milliseconds

    c. seconds

    d. mta

3. Which of these systems uses a binary logging system?

    a. syslogd

    b. journald

    c. rsyslogd

    d. klogd

4. Where can packages keep config files controlling their logging behavior?

    a. /etc/systemd/

    b. /etc/logrotate.d/

    c. /var/log/syslog/

    d. /etc/rsyslog.d/

5. Which packages do you need to install to get the postfix MTA working?

    a. mailutils and postfix

    b. sendmail and postfix

    c. exim and mailutils

    d. mailutils, postfix, and newaliases

6. Which file do you edit to change your e-mail domain information?

    a. /etc/mailutils/main.cf

    b. /etc/mail/mailutils/config.conf

    c. /etc/postfix/main.cf

    d. /etc/mail/postfix.conf

7. You can list all attached printers using:

    a. lp -d

    b. lp -ls

    c. lprm -

    d. lpq

Answer Key

1. d, 2. a, 3. b, 4. b, 5. a, 6. c, 7. d

■ ■ ■

## CHAPTER 9

Topic 109: Networking Fundamentals

Without a way to accurately identify how to reach devices, all network (and Internet) communication would simply collapse. My computer might be physically connected to yours (and to a million others), but expecting my e-mail to magically find its destination without a routable address is like throwing a bottle with a message inside into the ocean and expecting it to arrive on the kitchen table of a friend who lives ten thousand miles away. Within five minutes.

Fundamentals of Internet Protocols

Broadly speaking, modern networks rely on three conventions to solve the problem of addressing: transmission protocols (like TCP, UDP, and ICMP), network addressing (IPv4 and IPv6), and service ports.

Transmission Protocols

The Transmission Control Protocol (TCP) carries most web, e-mail, and ftp communication. It is TCP's packet verification feature that qualifies it for content that can't afford to arrive incomplete. The User Datagram Protocol (UDP) is a good choice for when verification isn't needed, as with streaming video and VOIP (Voice Over Internet Protocol), which can tolerate some dropped packets. UDP does provide checksums. The Internet Control Message Protocol (ICMP; part of the Internet layer of the Internet protocol suite, rather than the Transport layer) is used mostly for quick and dirty exchanges like ping.

Network Addressing

Every network-connected device must have its own unique IP (Internet Protocol) address. I'll discuss IPv6 addresses a bit later, but for now, let's work with IPv4.

© David Clinton 2016
D. Clinton, *Practical LPIC-1 Linux Certification Study Guide*,
DOI 10.1007/978-1-4842-2358-1_9

IPv4

An IPv4 address is made up of four numeric octets, each comprised of a number between 0 and 255, such as this:

```
192.168.0.101
```

Those four octets are divided into two parts: octets toward the left describe networks, and octets to the right describe individual nodes (each of which can be assigned to a single device). Put in slightly different terms, the network is the larger space within which local devices exist and communicate freely with each other. The nodes are those individual devices.

In one possible configuration of the above example, the first three octets (192.168.0) might have been set aside as the network, and the final octet (101) is the node address given to a particular device. Such a network could have as many as 256 devices (although at least three of those addresses—0, 255, and often 1—are reserved for network use).

This can be described either through a netmask, such as 255.255.255.0, or using the CIDR (Classless Inter-Domain Routing) convention, such as 192.168.0.0/24. The 24 in this case represents the network portion, made up of 24 bits, or three 8-bit octets (3*8=24).

However, the same address could actually be used for completely different network structures. Let's say, by way of an example, that our network will grow beyond 256 devices. We could reserve two octets for nodes rather than just one. In this case, only the first two octets would make up the network (subnet) address: 192.168, freeing the other two octets for nodes. This would make more than 65,000 (256*256) addresses available. Here's what the netmask of such an address would look like:

```
255.255.0.0
```

And here's how the same network would be represented using the CIDR format (remember: 2*8=16):

```
192.168.0.0/16
```

Let's go back to the original example (192.168.0.0/24). The third octet was, as you will remember, part of the network address. But you can use it to create multiple subnets. One subnet, allowing (around) 256 nodes, would be:

```
192.168.0
```

But you could create a second subnet that would allow a different set of (around) 256 nodes using this notation:

```
192.168.1
```

126

In fact, you could create more than 250 separate networks, each supporting more than 250 unique nodes, all the way up to:

```
192.168.254
```

Why would you want to do this? Because networking is about more than just connecting devices, it's also about managing and, sometimes, separating them. Perhaps your company has resources that need to be accessible to some people (the developers, perhaps) but not others (marketing). But marketing might need access to a whole different set of resources. Keeping them logically separated into their own subnets can be a super efficient way to do that.

One more point about subnetting: to make things just a bit more complicated, you can use addresses from a single octet for both networks and nodes. You could, for instance, reserve some of the third octet for networks and the rest for device nodes. It might look something like this in CIDR:

```
172.16.0.1/20
```

and would have a netmask of:

```
255.255.240.0
```

It takes a while to absorb these rules. As always, you'll learn quickest by playing with your own networks (I'll demonstrate the tools you can use for this later). In the meantime, by doing a Google search for "subnet calculator" you can find a number of terrific tools to help you visualize and design an infinite range of subnets.

Network Address Translation (NAT)

You may have noticed that my examples above were all either in the 192.168 or 172.16 address ranges. There's a reason for that (although the basic rules discussed will apply to all network addresses): these are within the address ranges reserved for local networks. Why do we need addresses that can be used only in local, private networks? Because if we didn't do that, we would have run out of network addresses many years ago.

The problem was that the Internet grew far larger than was ever imagined. The number of attached devices had grown into the billions (and now, with the growing Internet of Things, beyond even that). IPv4—by definition—can provide just over four billion theoretical addresses, and that's not nearly enough.

The brilliant solution adopted by Internet architects was to reserve certain address ranges for use **ONLY** in private networks that would communicate with the "outside" world by way of network translation at the router level. This way, you could have millions of devices behind a single physical or virtual router, each with its own privately routable address, but all together using only a single public address.

These are the three private NAT address ranges:

10.0.0.0	to	10.255.255.255
172.16.0.0	to	172.31.255.255
192.168.0.0	to	192.168.255.255

You should be aware that all IPv4 network addresses (not only NAT) fall into one of three classes:

Class:	First octet:
Class A	between 1 and 127
Class B	between 128 and 191
Class C	between 192 and 223

As you can see, each of the three NAT address ranges falls into a different network class. At the same time, I should mention that network class rules are no longer always strictly observed.

IPv6

The IPv6 protocol was a different solution to the problem of limited numbers of available addresses. Largely because of the success of NAT, there's been little pressure to widely adopt IPv6, so you won't see all that much of it yet. But its time will definitely come, and you should be familiar with how it works.

IPv6 addresses are 128-bit addresses and are made up of eight hexadecimal numbers separated by colons.

▓ **Note**   Hexadecimal numbers (sometimes called base 16 or hex) are simply numbers that use 0-9 (to represent the numbers 0-9), and the first six letters of the alphabet (a-f) representing the numbers 10-15.

This is what an IPv6 address might look like:

```
fd60:0:0:0:240:f8cf:fd51:67cf
```

For those addresses (like the one above) with more than one adjacent field equaling zero, you can also write it with compressed fields replaced by double colons:

```
fd60::240:f8cf:fd51:67cf
```

Just as discussed with IPv4, IPv6 addresses are divided into two parts: the network section (those fields to the left) and the address section (to the right). IPv6 notation, much like CIDR notation, distinguish between network and address fields using an /n value. Given that IPv6 addresses are 128-bit addresses, an address whose four leftmost fields represent networks would be /64, whereas an actual device would be designated as /128.

Service Ports

Even though every network-connected device has its own unique address, because a single server can offer multiple services, incoming traffic will also need to know which service port it wants. By accepted convention, all ports between 1 and 65535 are divided into three types:

1 to 1023	Well-known ports
1024 to 49151	ICANN registered ports (reserved for specific commercial protocols)
49152 to 65535	Dynamic ports (available to anyone for ad hoc use)

■ **Note** We should perhaps pause every now and again to appreciate the many conventions that "rule" the information technology world. Without accepted conventions, there really could be no Internet, or even much of an IT industry. It's especially noteworthy that many of our most important protocols were created through the hard work of very bright people acting as unpaid volunteers.

Table 9-1 lists some of the more common well-known ports with which you should be familiar, both for the LPIC exam and for daily your work as a Linux admin.

Table 9-1. *Common "Well-Known" Network Ports and the Services for Which They're Used*

Port	Uses
21	FTP data control
22	SSH (Secure Shell)
23	Telnet (useful, but not secure)
25	SMTP (Simple Mail Transfer Protocol)
53	DNS (Domain Name System)
80	HTTP (Hypertext Transfer Protocol)
110	POP3
123	NTP (Network Time Protocol)
139	NetBIOS
143	IMAP (Internet Message Access Protocol)
161	SNMP (Simple Network Management Protocol)
162	snmptrap # Traps for SNMP
389	LDAP (Lightweight Directory Access Protocol)
443	HTTPS (Hypertext Transfer Protocol over SSL)
465	URL Rendesvous Directory (Cisco)
514	(UDP) syslog
514	(TCP) cmd (no passwords)
636	LDAP over SSL
993	IMAPS (Internet Message Access Protocol over SSL)
995	POP3 over TLS/SSL

You can see a much more complete and up-to-date list of the well-known and ICANN (Internet Corporation for Assigned Names and Numbers) registered ports in the / etc/services file:

```
less /etc/services
```

Directing a request through a specific service port will often require that you add the port number to the target address. Thus, an HTTP request might look like this:

```
192.168.0.146:80
```

And a request for a service on an ad hoc port might use:

```
192.168.0.146:60123
```

Basic Network Configuration

Now that you are hopefully comfortable with the general principles of networking, let's turn our attention to the practical task of setting up and maintaining network connectivity.

First, I should point out that things are changing in Linuxland: the much-loved ifconfig family of commands from the net-tools package is being deprecated in favor of ip. Net-tools is still installed by default on many distributions, and it can always be installed manually, but the world is—slowly—moving toward ip. The LPIC exam, in its current form, requires knowledge of both systems, so I'll demonstrate them side by side.

You can run ifconfig on its own to see a list of all your recognized network devices and their statuses:

```
$ ifconfig
eth0      Link encap:Ethernet   HWaddr 74:d4:35:5d:4c:a5
      inet    addr:192.168.0.105
Bcast:192.168.0.255
Mask:255.255.255.0
      inet6 addr: fe80::76d4:35ff:fe5d:4ca5/64 Scope:Link
      UP BROADCAST RUNNING MULTICAST  MTU:1500  Metric:1
      RX packets:194338 errors:0 dropped:0 overruns:0 frame:0
      TX packets:136839 errors:0 dropped:0 overruns:0 carrier:0
      collisions:0 txqueuelen:1000
      RX bytes:191307800 (191.3 MB)    TX bytes:18732326 (18.7 MB)
```

In the case of this partial output, ifconfig shows us that the eth0 NIC has been given the DHCP NAT address of 192.168.0.105 and an IPv6 address. It also displays various other indicators, including the download and upload statistics since the last boot.

Using ip addr list produces a similar output, but with less scope:

```
ip addr list
2: eth0: <BROADCAST,MULTICAST,UP,LOWER_UP>
mtu 1500 qdisc pfifo_fast state UP group default qlen 1000
      link/ether 74:d4:35:5d:4c:a5 brd ff:ff:ff:ff:ff:ff
      inet 192.168.0.102/24 brd 192.168.0.255 scope global eth0
            valid_lft forever preferred_lft forever
         inet6 fe80::76d4:35ff:fe5d:4ca5/64 scope link
            valid_lft forever preferred_lft forever
```

If you're feeling lazy, you can accomplish the same thing using "ip a l" or even just "ip a".

If you don't see an interface that you thought should have been there, it might simply not have been loaded. You can help it along with this (assuming that its name is eth1):

```
sudo ifup eth1
```

In the brave new world of ip, this is how you would do the same thing:

```
sudo ip link set dev eth1 up
```

Let's parse this command: ip will use the set command against the device (dev) whose type is link that's identified as eth1, telling Linux to bring the device up. As you can see, ip syntax is a bit more like human speech.

You can bring a device down using either:

```
sudo ip link set dev eth1 down
```

or:

```
sudo ifdown eth1
```

I should add that, unlike ip link set, ifup and ifdown can also be used to configure (or deconfigure) interfaces.

You will sometimes have to configure an interface manually, which can be done from the command line. This example does it the ip way:

```
sudo ip a add 192.168.1.150/255.255.255.0 dev eth1
```

Here "ip a add" was used to tell the system that you're adding an interface and applying it to the known device, eth1. You assign this interface the IP address of 192.168.1.150 (making sure that it fits with the subnet architecture and will be able to connect to the router), using a netmask of 255.255.255.0. This can also be done by editing the configuration files.

On Fedora, you'll want to work with the appropriate file in the /etc/sysconfig/network-scripts directory. Here's a possible example:

```
nano /etc/sysconfig/network-scripts/ifcfg-enp2s0f0
```

On Debian/Ubuntu machines, it's the interfaces file that you're after:

```
nano /etc/network/interfaces
```

It's more common for interfaces to get their IP addresses automatically from a DHCP (Dynamic Host Configuration Protocol) server. This will often occur behind the scenes during system boot. If, for some reason, it didn't work for your interface, or if it's an interface you just added, you can send a request for a DHCP address using:

```
sudo dhclient eth1
```

For an interface to gain access to the larger network (and to the Internet beyond), it will need a route to the outside world, which will generally go through a router (hence the name). You can view your current route tables using:

```
route
```

If you don't yet have a working route and you do know the IP address of your router, you can add a route, using either:

```
sudo route add default gw 192.168.1.1
```

or:

```
sudo ip route add default via 192.168.1.1
```

By the way, an improperly set route table is a very common cause of network problems. If you've recently updated the address of your router or other gateway device and then suffer some connectivity problem, make sure your route table matches the real-world router.

Basic Network Troubleshooting

So nothing's working. Well, the workstations are all humming away happily, but your users aren't able to download their important productivity documents (and it's not like YouTube is down or anything). Your boss doesn't look very pleased about this and you want to know what to do first.

This is Linux, right? So you open a terminal. As you can see from Figure 9-1, I'll start from the inside and work out to troubleshoot.

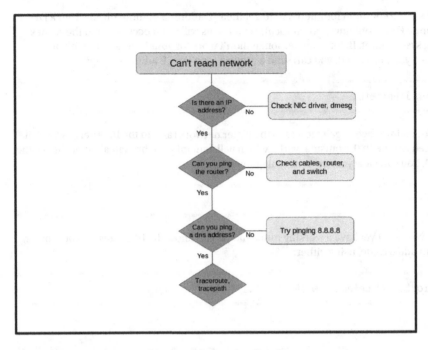

Figure 9-1. *Sample networking troubleshooting flowchart*

Check whether your computer's external interface (usually designated as either eth0 or em0) has an IP address:

```
ifconfig
```

or:

```
ip a
```

If it does, that probably means you've been successfully connected to your DHCP server, so the problem must lie farther afield. If you don't have an IP address, you might want to use dmesg to confirm that the network interface itself was picked up by your system:

```
dmesg | grep eth0
```

If there's no match for eth0 (or eth1, em0, or whatever you suspect might be the designation for your interface), then your kernel-level driver might have crashed (see Chapter 8 on kernel modules), or you might have a hardware problem of some sort.

You can shut down the machine and open the case to confirm that the network card (assuming that it isn't integrated with the motherboard) is properly seated in its slot. Remember to properly ground yourself. If that appears to be fine and you've got a spare card, you can install that to see if Linux recognizes it when you boot up again.

In any case, assuming you get through that stage without discovering what's causing your trouble, check to see if you can ping your router:

```
ping 192.168.0.1
```

Remember: your router address will usually be the same as your DHCP address, but with a 1 in the final field, rather than whatever number you had. Ping, by the way, uses the ICMP transmission protocol to send lots of very small data packets to the specified address, requesting that the host echoes the packets back. If ping was successful, you will be shown something like this:

```
PING 192.168.0.1 (192.168.0.1) 56(84) bytes of data.
64 bytes from 192.168.0.1: icmp_seq=1 ttl=57 time=26.2
64 bytes from 192.168.0.1: icmp_seq=2 ttl=57 time=25.9
64 bytes from 192.168.0.1: icmp_seq=3 ttl=57 time=26.7
64 bytes from 192.168.0.1: icmp_seq=4 ttl=57 time=26.9
```

■ **Note**   Don't forget that, as the industry moves to IPv6, more and more purpose-built tools will appear to accommodate that change. Ping6 is one of those.

If that works, then the problem is clearly not between your computer and the router. If that doesn't work, then you should check your cabling and switches at all ends. You can also try rebooting your router and switch.

■ **Note**   It sometimes feels like 95% of IT problems can be solved by rebooting. Most of the remaining 5% can be taken care of by keeping users away from IT resources, although that may sometimes lead to long-term productivity complications.

Now let's assume that you can successfully ping your router. The problem must be a bit farther out. Try pinging the DNS name for a known web site:

```
ping google.com
```

If that fails, there might be a problem with your Internet provider (which will require a friendly phone call, assuming your phone still works). But it's also possible that your DNS address translation isn't working. To find out, ping the IP address of an external service that you know should work. My favorite for these times is Google's DNS server, because the IP is just so easy to remember:

```
ping 8.8.8.8
```

If that works (even though *ping google.com* did not), then you know it's a DNS issue, which is discussed in the last section of this chapter.

If it doesn't work, it might be your Internet provider's fault, but it can still be helpful to narrow down the location of the blockage. Traceroute (or its IPv6 cousin, traceroute6) can help fill in some of the gaps. Running traceroute against a known address will show you each step your packets took along the route to a destination, including the one right before things failed:

```
traceroute 8.8.8.8
```

Tracepath, by the way, delivers much the same function as traceroute. And both traceroute and tracepath have their IPv6 equivalents: traceroute6 and tracepath6.

If the network problem is inbound, rather than outbound (in other words: people can't access resources on your network), then you'll need a different set of tools. First, you should confirm that all necessary ports are open. So, for instance, if you're running a web server, you'll probably need to open port 80 and, perhaps, 443.

You can use netstat to display all the ports and sockets that are currently listening on your system:

```
netstat -l | grep http
```

Using grep http will, of course, help narrow down your search.

From a computer on an external network you can also use netcat to poke at your network to see what's open. This example will test port 80 (assuming that "your network" is bootstrap-it.com):

```
nc -z -v bootstrap-it.com 80
```

In general, by the way, netcat is an excellent tool for testing your security.

Configure Client Side DNS

As mentioned earlier, all network devices have unique IP addresses. Since, however, people find it a lot easier to work with and remember more human-readable addresses (like bootstrap-it.com), DNS (Domain Name System) servers will translate back and forth between IPs and URLs. When I type *google.com* into the URL bar of a browser, there's a DNS server somewhere that's busy converting that into the correct IP address and sending off my request.

For this to work, you will need to designate a DNS server that can handle translation requests. This can be done on Debian/Ubuntu machines from the file:

```
/etc/network/interfaces
```

and, on Red Hat, using if-up scripts.

Here's what an interfaces file with DNS settings might look like:

```
auto eth0
iface eth0 inet static
    address 10.0.0.23
    netmask 255.255.255.0
    gateway 10.0.0.1
    dns-nameservers 208.67.222.222 208.67.220.220
    dns-search example.com
```

The nameservers being used here are those provided by the OpenDNS service.

The dns-search line tells the system that any searches launched without fully qualified domain names (FQDNs) will be appended to example.com.

Let me explain what that means: if I were to enter just the word "documents" into the URL bar of a browser, the request would normally fail. That's because there is no domain that matches *documents* (and it's a badly formed address in any case). However, with my dns-search value set, the local DNS server would try to find a resource somewhere within the local network called example.com/documents and dutifully fetch that for me.

Often, however, if your machine is a DHCP client, it will take the DNS settings) from its DHCP server. You might see a reference to this in the /etc/resolv.conf file (which, these days, is really nothing more than an autogenerated symlink):

```
# Generated by NetworkManager
search d-linkrouter
nameserver 192.168.0.1
```

The hostname of your own computer can also be used as an alternate to its IP address. You can update your host name by editing both the /etc/hosts and /etc/hostname files.

The hosts file can also be used to create a local alias. Let's say that, for some reason, you need to type commands in the terminal involving long URLs:

```
wget amazon.com
```

Okay. So amazon.com is not a particularly long URL, but you understand what I mean. If you'd like to create a shortcut, add this line to your hosts file:

```
54.239.25.200    www.amazon.com    a
```

From now on, whenever you need to access amazon.com from the command line, typing just the letter "a" will get it done:

```
wget a
```

The host and dig tools can be run against either domain names or IP addresses to return DNS information. Both can be useful for troubleshooting DNS problems:

```
$ host bootstrap-it.com
```

The order your system uses when resolving hostnames to IP addresses is determined by the hosts line in the /etc/nsswitch.conf file. Here's an example:

```
hosts:  files myhostname mdns4_minimal [NOTFOUND=return]
dns mdns4
```

You can edit the order the system) uses by simply changing the sequence of this line.

Now Try This

If you can get your hands on an unused wireless router, plug it in to your PC via a network cable and log in to the interface (it usually works by pointing your browser to 192.168.0.1, you can check the router case for login details). Note the current LAN settings (and, if you're nervous, how to reset it to its factory settings).

Now change the network subnet mask (which will, most likely, be 255.255.255.0) to 255.255.0.0, and create a network in a new subnet. You might want to use a range that's something like 192.168.1.1 to 192.168.1.253. Boot a laptop or a smartphone and log it in as a DHCP client on the new network. Make sure the IP address now used by your device is within the range you set.

Warning: be prepared to do a lot of rebooting and reconfiguring until you get it right. Remember: It's not frustrating, it's fun!

Test Yourself

1. The ping travels using the _____ protocol:

   a. TCP

   b. ICMP

   c. CIDR

   d. UDP

2. A subnet with a CIDR of 172.16.0.1/18 would have which netmask?

   a. 255.255.240.0

   b. 255.255.255.0

    c.   255.255.255.18

    d.   255.255.192.0

3.   Which of the following addresses belongs to Class B?

    a.   172.30.1.126

    b.   192.15.0.54

    c.   10.0.0.2

    d.   198.168.1.1

4.   Which of these can't possibly be a real IPv6 address?

    a.   fd60:0:0:0:240:r8cf:fd51:67cf

    b.   fd60:0:0:0:240:f8cf:fd51:67cf

    c.   fd60::240:f8cf:fd51:67cf

    d.   fd60:0:0:0:240:f8cf:fd51:6776

5.   Which of these will successfully connect to a secure http web page?

    a.   `https://bootstrap-it.com:22`

    b.   `https://bootstrap-it.com:443`

    c.   `https://bootstrap-it.com:80`

    d.   `https://bootstrap-it.com:143`

6.   **Which of these will start a network interface?**

    a.   ip link set dev eth0 down

    b.   ifup eth0

    c.   ifconfig eth0

    d.   dhclient eth0

7.   Which of these will NOT tell you whether an interface is functioning?

    a.   ifconfig

    b.   ip a

    c.   dmesg | grep eth0

    d.   ping eth0

8. Which of these will NOT tell you which network service ports are open?

   a. netstat -l

   b. netstat

   c. nc -z -v bootstrap-it 80

   d. traceroute bootstrap-it 80

9. Which of these has NOTHING to do with DNS servers?

   a. /etc/NetworkManager/NetworkManager.conf

   b. /etc/network/interfaces

   c. /etc/resolv.conf

   d. /etc/nsswitch.conf

Answer Key

1. b, 2. d, 3. a, 4. a, 5. b, 6. b, 7. d, 8. d, 9. Trick question: they ALL do!

CHAPTER 10

■ ■ ■

Topic 110: Security

Creating a reasonably secure compute environment requires elements from just about every area of system administration. Perhaps that's why the LPI put security at the very end of their exam objectives, because you will, in fact, need all your skills to make this work.

I used the term "reasonably secure" because, when it comes to security, anyone who thinks his resources are 100% safe is fooling himself. An old friend who had worked for a national foreign service once told me that every single one of that country's overseas embassies was provided with a government-issue hammer for use in the event they were overrun. The purpose of the hammer? To physically destroy every hard drive in the building. There really is no better solution (and even that one is imperfect).

The bottom line: when it comes to IT security, there's never enough that can be done and you can never completely relax. Let's get started.

System Security

As discussed previously, user passwords are usually among the weakest links in your system. In Chapter 7, I explained how you can use the command chage to force your users to update their passwords from time to time. While it's not required by the LPIC-1 exam, you can also use PAM (Pluggable Authentication Module) to enforce password complexity. PAM is controlled through the /etc/pam.d/system-auth file (on Red Hat) or the /etc/pam.d/common- password (on Debian systems). Editing the "password required" line to read something like this:

```
password required pam_cracklib.so minlen=12 lcredit=1
ucredit=1 dcredit=2 ocredit=1
```

can make a big difference. This example will force users to create passwords whose minimum length is 12 characters, and where "credit" is given for the presence of at least one character that's in lowercase, one in uppercase, two digits, and one "other" (i.e., nonalphanumeric).

I also discussed how important it is to use a root or admin account as seldom as possible. Administrative powers should be given to only those users who absolutely need it, and even then, they should use those powers only through sudo.

© David Clinton 2016
D. Clinton, *Practical LPIC-1 Linux Certification Study Guide*,
DOI 10.1007/978-1-4842-2358-1_10

You can add a user to the sudo group (thereby giving him the right to admin powers for single commands) through chmod:

```
sudo usermod -aG sudo steve
```

This will add a user named Steve to the sudo group. Once you've done that, you can view the /etc/group file and Steve's name should be among those on the sudo line.

```
cat /etc/group | grep sudo
```

You can edit the way that sudo works on your system through the /etc/sudoers file, but you must use the visudo command rather than trying to edit the file directly. If you view the sudoers file (which itself, for obvious reasons, requires sudo), you will notice that there are separate lines defining the privileges given to members of the root, admin, and sudo groups. This allows you to very finely tune the powers you give to each of your administrative users. An example of this would be:

```
# User privilege specification
root    ALL=(ALL:ALL) ALL
# Members of the admin group may gain root privileges
%admin ALL=(ALL) ALL
# Allow members of group sudo to execute any command
%sudo  ALL=(ALL:ALL) ALL
```

So, to review, you should never, ever, EVER log in to a system as root or with persistent admin powers. And that's perfectly true, except where it isn't. There will be times when you have no choice but to start up an admin shell. To do that, type:

```
sudo su
```

and enter your password. Note that, in most cases, your shell prompt will now look something like this:

```
root@newpc:/home#
```

You should also keep track of the users who are logging in to your system. If, for instance, most of the gang where you work are out of the office by five each afternoon, then you should expect there won't be too many of them still logged in a half an hour later. And even if one or two might have left their workstations running (hopefully with a password-protected screensaver), you definitely won't be seeing too much activity.

That's why a quick review of user log ins can be useful. Using "w" will tell you when a user logged in, what system resources he's using, and, most importantly, what process he's running at the moment. Here is an example:

```
$ w
12:48:00 up  4:49,  3 users,  load average: 0.02, 0.18, 0.30
USER      TTY       FROM              LOGIN@   IDLE    JCPU
PCPU WHAT
dbclinto :0        :0                08:00   ?xdm?   32:40
0.22s init --user
dbclinto pts/1     :0.0              09:26   21.00s  0.28s
0.16s ssh dbclinton@1
dbclinto pts/4     :0.0              12:47   0.00s   0.06s
0.01s w
```

This output shows you that, besides my own bootup log in from 8:00 this morning, I've also got two shell sessions running: one, an ssh session into the Fedora laptop right next to me (it sure beats having to turn my chair around to actually use its keyboard), and the other, the shell from which I ran w.

Doesn't look like anyone else is around, and that's what I want to see. I need to be able to account for every single session that's listed.

Running who and last will also list log ins. Last can be particularly useful, as it lists all of the log ins since the beginning of the current month. Adding -d will also show you the origin host of each log in to give you an idea of where they've been coming from:

```
last -d
```

Monitoring files using lsof (LiSt Open Files) can also be a powerful security tool, especially since, in Linux, everything (even a directory) is a file.

You can list all processes (and their users) that have opened a specific file:

```
lsof /var/log/syslog
```

By adding +D, you can list all open files within a directory hierarchy:

```
lsof +D /var/log/
```

Using -u will narrow down your search to only those files opened by the specified user:

```
lsof -u steve
```

But suppose you're Steve and you know (or at least you hope) you're reliable, but you'd like to check into all those other suspicious characters you've seen around. The use of the caret symbol (^) will display everyone **EXCEPT** you:

```
lsof -u ^steve
```

You can use lsof along with kill to close all files opened by a specific user:

```
kill -9 `lsof -t -u steve`
```

You can even use lsof (with -i) to list all open network connections:

```
lsof -i
```

Consider incorporating some of those lsof tools into a script to automatically monitor your system activity.

Much of the same functionality of lsof can also be found in fuser. Fuser, too, will let you zero in on specific files:

```
fuser /var/log/syslog
```

It must be added, however, that fuser can get much more personal about it. Using:

```
fuser -km /home
```

will kill all processes accessing the filesystem /home. Be warned: by kill, it means kill.

By displaying which users and processes are accessing the http port (80), this next example will tell you if there's any unauthorized activity involving your web server:

```
sudo fuser -v -n tcp 80
```

In Chapter 9 you used netcat and netstat to search for open network ports. As mentioned there, from a security perspective, you should always be very interested in making sure there are no unnecessary ports open on the sites you manage. There's one more tool that covers some of the same ground: nmap. Running nmap against local or Internet-based addresses will display all open ports:

```
nmap bootstrap-it.com
```

Using nmap with the -sU flag will perform a UDP scan:

```
sudo nmap -sU 10.0.2.143
```

You can restrict an nmap scan to a specific port:

```
nmap -p 80 bootstrap-it.com
```

or, if you're trying to monitor a larger number of network resources, you can scan a range of addresses, with built-in exclusions:

```
nmap 192.168.2.0/24 --exclude 192.168.2.3
```

Besides looking for unusual things that are going on right now, you should also keep an eye open for vulnerabilities that could be exploited in the future. Files with suid permissions comprise one class of files that can potentially cause trouble.

As mentioned previously, a file with the suid bit can be used by any user AS THOUGH they shared the file's full admin rights. Sometimes, as with the /usr/bin/passwd binary, this is necessary. However, if you notice the suid in unexpected places, you should consider taking a closer look.

You can easily check your whole filesystem for suid using:

```
sudo find / -type f -perm -u=s -ls
```

Nice. The problem is that this will probably return a rather long list of files. How are you to know if there's actually a problem? One solution is to take the stream produced by using find and filter it for entries that are also writable by others, have the sgid bit set, or are unowned by a valid package or user. That will narrow down your search to combinations that definitely deserve more attention.

You can search for files with guid (group) permissions using:

```
sudo find / -type f -perm -g=s -ls
```

And this will find ownerless files:

```
find / -xdev \( -nouser -o -nogroup \) -print
```

You can set limits on the system resources available to specified users or even groups using ulimit. Try reviewing your own default limits by running:

```
ulimit -a
```

Notice the categories that can be controlled, including individual file size, the number of open files, and the maximum number of user processes. Maintaining the right balance of limits can help prevent the abuse of account privileges without unnecessarily restricting your users' legitimate activities. You can edit user and group limits in the /etc/security/limits.conf file. Here are some of the sample settings that illustrate the way the file works:

```
#root          hard    core        100000
#@student      hard    nproc       20
```

145

```
#@faculty        soft    nproc            20
#@faculty        hard    nproc            50
#@student        -       maxlogins        4
```

You should also keep an eye on active processes using ps:

```
ps aux
```

Of course, that will produce way too much information to be useful. Adding our old friend grep into the mix should help narrow things down:

```
ps aux | grep apache2
```

Host Security

Besides controlling the behavior of local users, it's also vital to be able to limit the things that people coming from beyond your local system can do. At its simplest, that might mean preventing nonroot log ins. Creating a readable file called nologin in the /etc directory will do just that:

```
sudo touch /etc/nologin
```

You can leave the file empty or include a message you'd like users to see that explains why they're currently locked out of the system.

Once you do decide to allow remote log ins, you can, in association with the init.d run-level control system I discussed in Chapter 1, closely control what your guests can do through the inetd (or, on newer distributions, xinetd) system. Inetd is known as a super-server because its job is to listen for requests on all ports listed in the config file and then, when appropriate, start and stop requested services.

The original goal was to save system resources by having one single running server activate services only when they were actually needed, and then shut them down when they're done. But, besides the built-in security benefits of turning off unused services, inetd also provided an added advantage through the ability to apply access control.

A typical /etc/xinetd.conf configuration file will include entries like these:

```
defaults
{
    instances         = 60
    log_type          = SYSLOG        authpriv
    log_on_success    = HOST PID
```

```
        log_on_failure      = HOST
        cps                 = 25 30
}
includedir /etc/xinetd.d
```

Note the includedir /etc/xinetd.d line, which points to the /etc/xinetd.d directory, which itself contains individual files for each service that will be controlled by xinetd. Here's an example of an xinetd file:

```
# default: off
# description: An RFC 863 discard server.
# This is the tcp version.
service discard
{
        disable         = yes
        type            = INTERNAL
        id              = discard-stream socket_type = stream
        protocol        = tcp
        user            = root
        wait            = no
}
# This is the udp version. service discard
{
        disable         = yes
        type            = INTERNAL
        id              = discard-dgram
        socket_type     = dgram
        protocol        = udp
        user            = root
        wait            = yes
}
```

The main value you should be aware of is disable. The current setting for both the TCP and UDP versions is "yes," which means that remote requests for the RFC 863 discard server will be refused. To tell xinetd to accept such requests, the disable value should be changed to "no." Discard, by the way, is roughly the equivalent of the /dev/null directory, a convenient place to dump debugging or testing data that will be immediately destroyed.

Besides discard and the few others you might see in a clean install of Linux, xinetd is also often used to control services like ftp, pop3, rsync, smtp, and telnet.

Once you've enabled a service through xinetd, anyone logging in will be able to launch it. If you'd like to retain control over exactly which remote users get to use a particular service, you should use TCP wrappers. To do that, you'll need to edit the appropriate service file in /etc/xinetd.d/ to tell xinetd to load the tcpd daemon, rather than the service daemon itself. As an example, here's what you would add to the vsftpd file:

147

```
server              = /usr/sbin/tcpd
serverargs          = /usr/sbin/vsftpd
```

You would also need to permit remote access by editing the disable line to read *no* rather than *yes*:

```
disable             = no
```

Any edits to the xinetd configuration require a service restart. If you're using Upstart, run:

```
sudo service xinetd restart
```

For Systemd, use this instead:

```
systemctl reload xinetd.service
```

Now you'll need to edit the hosts.allow and hosts.deny files in the /etc/ directory. You could, for instance, add this line to hosts.deny:

```
vsftpd:    ALL
```

which will deny access to users logging in from any external host. The hosts.deny file will be read first, allowing the contents of hosts.allow the last word. Therefore, if you would add something like this to the hosts.allow file:

```
vsftpd:    192.168.0.101, 10.0.4.23
```

then users coming from specifically those two hosts WOULD be allowed.

Encryption: Securing Data in Transit

Files often need to be moved from place to place. If it's just family photos or recipes, you might as well simply send them as e-mail attachments or via ftp (or fax, for those of you old enough to remember such things, although your family photos might not come through the fax at quite their original resolution).

But you should be aware that data packets moving across the Internet are—legally or otherwise—visible to just about anyone who cares to look. For that reason, you should never transfer files containing financial or other private information (including credit card numbers or passwords) through wireless or public digital networks, unless they've been encrypted first.

Encryption rewrites a data file using an encryption algorithm that makes the file unintelligible. If the encryption was strong enough, the only practical way to decrypt it and get access to its contents is to apply the public half of a decryption key pair that essentially performs the encryption process in reverse. Many network communication tools—like telnet, ftp, and most e-mail services—are **not** encrypted and are, therefore, vulnerable.

Now let's look at using the OpenSSH secure shell for encrypted remote login sessions (something I've used a fair number of times already through the demonstrations in this book), and learn about SSH tunnels and encrypting specific files using GnuPG.

OpenSSH

Once the OpenSSH server package is installed on a computer, it can host remote login sessions:

```
sudo apt-get install openssh-server
```

Users who only need to log on to remote systems as guests can install the client package:

```
sudo apt-get install openssh-client
```

Once everything is properly installed, a user can open a new session using the ssh command and enter the password when prompted:

```
ssh tony@10.0.4.243
tony@10.0.4.243's password:
```

All keystrokes and data that travel back and forth for the duration of this session will be securely encrypted. You can also transfer files between sites using the scp ("secure copy") program that's included with OpenSSH:

```
scp myfile.tar.gz tony@10.0.4.243:/home/tony/
```

Note that you will need to specify a target directory on the remote computer where you'd like the file saved. The target directory has to be one to which the user you're logging in as has access. That means you won't be able to copy a file directly to, say, the /var/www/html/ directory of the remote machine.

You can also use scp the other way, to move a file from a remote host to yours. This will copy the newfile.tar.gz file to the current directory (represented by the dot at the end):

```
scp tony@10.0.4.243:/home/tony/newfile.tar.gz .
```

The /etc/ssh/ssh_config file controls the way local users will access remote hosts, while the /etc/ssh/sshd_config file (assuming that openssh- server is installed) manages how remote users log in to your machine. Running *ls* against the /etc/ssh/ directory will display the key pairs ssh uses to authenticate sessions:

```
        $ ls /etc/ssh
moduli          ssh_host_dsa_key        ssh_host_ecdsa_key.pub
ssh_import_id
ssh_config      ssh_host_dsa_key.pub    ssh_host_rsa_key
sshd_config     ssh_host_ecdsa_key      ssh_host_rsa_key.pub
```

Those keys with a .pub extension are public keys, while the versions without an extension are private keys. This directory includes key pairs using the DSA, ECDSA, RSA, and ed25519 encryption algorithms.

OpenSSH version 1 would probably have used key pair files called ssh_host_rsa and ssh_host_dsa. There are other differences between versions 1 and 2. With version 1, for instance, once the client receives the public key from the server, it would use the server's public key to generate and then send a 256-bit secret key. Now that they both have an identical secret key, the two systems can safely share data. Version 2, on the other hand, will use what's called a Diffie-Hellman key agreement to negotiate a secret key without needing to send any complete key over the network.

Passwordless Access

Even OpenSSH has a potential weakness, and it's an old, familiar complaint: the password. Based on the discussion in previous chapters, you still need to authenticate to the host system using a password.

Besides the inconvenience, this extra step also introduces something of a vulnerability into the process. Therefore, wherever possible, you should configure your ssh connections for passwordless access. You do this by generating a new key pair on your client machine (the computer you plan to use to connect to the server):

```
ssh-keygen -t rsa
```

You'll need to choose a specific algorithm type: the above example uses rsa. You can optionally create a passphrase that you'll use later whenever you log in. In any case, using a passphrase is not required and it's often ignored.

The passphrase should not be confused with the host account password, as this one simply locally decrypts the private key and does not require sending account passwords over a network connection.

The new key pair will be saved to the hidden .ssh directory within your user's home directory. You can view the files through ls with the -a (meaning all) option:

```
ls -a ~/.ssh
```

Now you will have to copy the new public key to the host. Remember: you should only do this using a secure transfer method:

```
scp keyname.pub tony@10.0.4.243:/home/tony
```

Log in to the host machine and add the contents of the new key to the ~/.ssh/authorized_keys file within the home directory of the account you will be accessing:

```
cat keyname.pub >> ~/.ssh/authorized_keys
```

If you do decide to pipe it in this way, make sure to use two greater than signs (>>) rather than one, as > will overwrite the file's current contents!

Next, still on the host machine, make sure that the authorized_keys file can be read ONLY by its owner:

```
chmod 600 ~/.ssh/authorized_keys
```

You can now log out of the host. Now for the fun part: try logging in once again:

```
ssh tony@10.0.4.243
```

You should get in without the need for a password. I'll bet that makes you feel really welcome!

Using ssh-agent

You can maintain a higher level of password security without needing to use (or expose) your passwords with each new session you initiate by employing ssh-agent. Running eval within a shell will pass a passphrase to OpenSSH each time you launch a new ssh session from within that shell.

```
eval `ssh-agent -s `
```

Note the use of the backtick (`) symbol, which is usually found at the top left corner of your keyboard.

You can then add your ssh key to the agent using:

```
ssh-add ~/.ssh/id_rsa
```

where id_rsa is the name of the key you wish to add.

X11 Tunnels

You can use ssh connectivity as a platform, or, as it's sometimes known, a tunnel, for a wider range of connected services. So, for instance, you can make remote use of the graphic functionality of an X11 session on top of an existing ssh session. Let's do that step by step.

On the host machine, edit the /etc/ssh/sshd_config file so that the value of the X11Forwarding line is yes:

```
sudo nano /etc/ssh/sshd_config
X11Forwarding yes
```

On the client machine (i.e., the PC you will use to log in to the host), edit the ForwardX11 line in the /etc/ssh/ssh_config file so that it, too, reads yes:

```
sudo nano /etc/ssh/ssh_config
ForwardX11 yes
```

Now, from your client computer, use ssh to start an X session:

```
ssh -X -l tony 10.0.4.243
```

You will find yourself in what looks like just another terminal session. What's so X about this? Don't trust me? Try running a GUI program like gedit (a graphic text editor):

```
gedit
```

If everything worked the way it should, you will find yourself using gedit on your laptop or workstation, but as part of the filesystem, and relying on the resources of your host. Depending on your network connection and memory limits, you might be surprised at the kinds of tasks you can attempt using such tunnels.

GnuPG Config

Our last stop on this journey will be file encryption. While encrypting networked sessions is a perfectly good solution, there may be times when all you want to do is send a single document containing some sensitive information. Rather than encrypting the whole connection, you can simply encrypt the document itself and provide your recipient with the key to decrypt it at the other end.

GPG (Gnu Privacy Guard) will encrypt a file using one or more public keys. The file can subsequently be decrypted using a private key that corresponds to any one of the public keys used during encryption. So, as illustrated in Figure 10-1, you could choose to generate a random symmetric key using the public key from the recipient's computer to get things started. It will then encrypt the file and send it, along with the new symmetric key. At the receiving end, GPG will use the recipient's private key to decrypt the message.

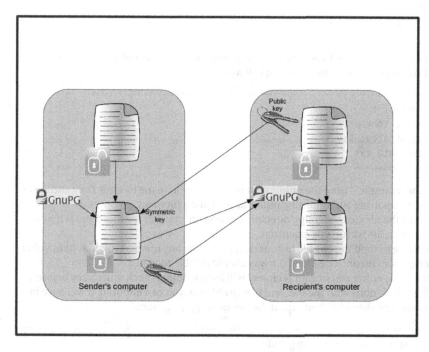

Figure 10-1. *The Gnu Guard key exchange process*

You could also use your own public key for encryption and then send it to your recipients for decryption.

You generate keys using gpg --genkey:

```
gpg --gen-key
```

The program will prompt you for a key type, key length, lifetime (i.e., when, if ever, the key will automatically expire), a username that you can create (and remember for later use), an e-mail address, a comment, and finally, a passphrase. Many of these details are used to help build randomness into the encryption.

The final step will be to produce "noise" (random keystrokes) while GPG generates the encrypted file. GPG expects a LOT of noise, so just hitting a few keys here and there might not do it. What I do is open a new shell (on the same machine, obviously), and create some industrial strength (but harmless) noise using something like this:

```
sudo find / -type f | xargs grep somerandomstring > /dev/null
```

Alternatively, you can install and run the haveged program to quiety generate all the entropy you need. Once it's done, you can go to the hidden GPG directory within your home directory and take a look:

```
cd ~/.gnupg
```

Once you've oriented yourself, it's time to encrypt a file. Assuming there's a file named verysecretdata.txt, here's how it will work:

```
gpg --encrypt \
--recipient tony-key \
--recipient steve-key \
verysecretdata.txt
```

In this example, I used the public keys previously sent to me by both Tony and Steve. I'll discuss importing and exporting public keys in just a moment.

Listing the files in the .gnupg directory once again, you can see that there is now a verysecretdata file with a .gpg extension.

Feel free to send the gpg file to your recipient using any method you like. Remember: it's encrypted so no one else along the way should be able to read it.

Of course, either you or your recipient will have to import each other's key before anything can be done with the file. And before either of you can import it, it will have to be exported and then sent. You export the key using gpg --export:

```
gpg --export username > mygpg.pub
```

The file name you use doesn't matter, as long as it has a .pub extension. Once you've transferred the key to the recipient, they can import it using gpg --import:

```
gpg --import mygpg.pub
```

Assuming that the key is now part of the recipient's GPG collection, they can decrypt it using some variation of this command, where the output value is the name you'd like the decrypted file to have and the value of decrypt is the encrypted file you've received:

```
gpg --output      verysecretdata      --decrypt
verysecretdata.txt.gpg
```

You can view all the keys that are currently part of your system using:

```
gpg --list-keys
```

And, as might sometimes be necessary, you can revoke a key with the key ID that you saw displayed by --list-keys:

```
gpg --gen-revoke 6372552D
```

Using --gen-revoke will generate some output, which you should copy into a file that you can keep safe, as it could prove very useful later. With the file, you will always be able to import your up-to-date key status into a new (or recovery) GPG installation. You import a file using:

```
gpg --import revoked.txt
```

The distribution and updating of keys between users can be managed through online public keyservers. You can retrieve a key using –recv-key and send it with –send-key. Here's what a retrieval command might look like:

```
gpg --keyserver certserver.pgp.com --recv-key 0xBB7576AC
```

Now Try This

Use ssh-keygen to set up passwordless access to a machine (perhaps an LXC container) and try it out to make sure it works. Now, while logged in on that machine, launch a full battery of tests against your own computer, testing for open ports, X access, and remote login access.

If you can't get through your own defenses, pat yourself on the back.

Test Yourself

1. Restricting the output of fuser to a specific port requires which flag?

    a. -v

    b. -i

    c. -sU

    d. -n

2. Which of these will find all files on the system with the guid bit set?

   a.   find / -type f -perm -u=s -ls

   b.   find / -xdev \(-nouser -o -nogroup \) -print

   c.   find / -type d -perm -u=s -ls

   d.   find / -type f -perm -g=s -ls

3. Which of these will list all open files beneath the specified directory?

   a.   lsof +D /var/log/

   b.   lsof -u /var/log/

   c.   lsof /var/log/

   d.   fuser /var/log/syslog

4. Which of these will using "w" NOT display?

   a.   Log in time.

   b.   Inode limit.

   c.   Origin host.

   d.   Idle time.

5. Which file is used to control inetd behavior?

   a.   /etc/xinetd.conf

   b.   /var/inetd.conf

   c.   /etc/inetd.conf

   d.   /etc/inetd.d/conf

6. Which lines must you edit in vsftpd to tell xinetd to control access?

   a.   Server and serverargs

   b.   Disable and server

   c.   Server and disable

   d.   User and serverargs

7. Which of these files controls the behavior of an ssh server?

   a. /etc/ssh/ssh_config

   b. /etc/ssh/ssh_host_dsa_key

   c. /etc/sshd_config

   d. /etc/ssh/sshd_config

8. The public key stored on a server requires which permissions?

   a. 644

   b. 600

   c. 640

   d. 755

9. Which config file should include ForwardX11 yes to allow X11 sessions?

   a. /etc/ssh/sshd_config

   b. /etc/sshd_config

   c. /etc/sshd/ssh_config

   d. /etc/ssh/ssh_config

10. Which will decrypt a GPG-encrypted file named my-encrypted-file.gpg?

   a. gpg --output newfilename --decrypt my-encrypted-file.gpg

   b. gpg --output my-encrypted-file.gpg --decrypt newfilename

   c. gpg --export my-encrypted-file.gpg > newfilename

   d. gpg --export newfilename > my-enctrypted-file.gpg

Answer Key

1. d, 2. d, 3. a, 4. b, 5. c, 6. a, 7. d, 8. b, 9. d, 10. a

APPENDIX

■ ■ ■

LPIC-1 Exam Objectives

(Taken from www.lpi.org/study-resources/lpic-1-101-exam-objectives)

LPIC-1 Exam 101

Exam Objectives Version: Version 4.0 (last updated: April 15th, 2015)
   Exam Covered: LPIC-1 101 (101-400) also available as CompTIA Linux+ (LX0-103); Exam 1 of 2 to obtain LPIC-1 Linux Server Professional certification

Topic 101: System Architecture

101.1 Determine and configure hardware settings
   Weight: 2
   Description: Candidates should be able to determine and configure fundamental system hardware.
   Key Knowledge Areas:

- Enable and disable integrated peripherals

- Configure systems with or without external peripherals such as keyboards

- Differentiate between the various types of mass storage devices

- Know the differences between coldplug and hotplug devices

- Determine hardware resources for devices

- Tools and utilities to list various hardware information (e.g., lsusb, lspci, etc.)

- Tools and utilities to manipulate USB devices

- Conceptual understanding of sysfs, udev, dbus

© David Clinton 2016
D. Clinton, *Practical LPIC-1 Linux Certification Study Guide*,
DOI 10.1007/978-1-4842-2358-1

The following is a partial list of the used files, terms and utilities:

modprobe	lsmod
/proc/	lspci
/dev/	lsusb

101.2 Boot the system
Weight: 3
Description: Candidates should be able to guide the system through the booting process.

Key Knowledge Areas:

- Provide common commands to the boot loader and options to the kernel at boot time

- Demonstrate knowledge of the boot sequence from BIOS to boot completion

- Understanding of SysVinit and systemd

- Awareness of Upstart

- Check boot events in the log files

Terms and Utilities:

dmesg	initramfs
BIOS	init
bootloader	SysVinit
kernel	systemd

101.3 Change runlevels/boot targets and shutdown or reboot system
Weight: 3
Description: Candidates should be able to manage the SysVinit runlevel or systemd boot target of the system. This objective includes changing to single user mode, shutdown or rebooting the system. Candidates should be able to alert users before switching runlevels/boot targets and properly terminate processes. This objective also includes setting the default SysVinit runlevel or systemd boot target. It also includes awareness of Upstart as an alternative to SysVinit or systemd.

Key Knowledge Areas:

- Set the default runlevel or boot target

- Change between runlevels/boot targets including single user mode

- Shutdown and reboot from the command line

- Alert users before switching runlevels/boot targets or other major system events

- Properly terminate processes

Terms and Utilities:

/etc/inittab	telinit	/usr/lib/ systemd/
shutdown	systemd	wall
init	systemctl	
/etc/init.d/	/etc/systemd/	

Topic 102: Linux Installation and Package Management

102.1 Design hard disk layout
Weight: 2
Description: Candidates should be able to design a disk partitioning scheme for a Linux system.
Key Knowledge Areas:

- Allocate filesystems and swap space to separate partitions or disks

- Tailor the design to the intended use of the system

- Ensure the /boot partition conforms to the hardware architecture requirements for booting

- Knowledge of basic features of LVM

Terms and Utilities:

/ (root) filesystem	swap space
/var filesystem	mount points
/home filesystem	partitions
/boot filesystem	

161

102.2 Install a boot manager

Weight: 2

Description: Candidates should be able to select, install and configure a boot manager.

Key Knowledge Areas:

- Providing alternative boot locations and backup boot options

- Install and configure a boot loader such as GRUB Legacy

- Perform basic configuration changes for GRUB 2

- Interact with the boot loader

The following is a partial list of the used files, terms and utilities:

```
menu.lst, grub.cfg and grub.conf
grub-install
grub-mkconfig
MBR
```

102.3 Manage shared libraries

Weight: 1

Description: Candidates should be able to determine the shared libraries that executable programs depend on and install them when necessary.

Key Knowledge Areas:

- Identify shared libraries

- Identify the typical locations of system libraries

- Load shared libraries

Terms and Utilities:

ldd	/etc/ld.so.conf
ldconfig	LD_LIBRARY_PATH

102.4 Use Debian package management

Weight: 3

Description: Candidates should be able to perform package management using the Debian package tools.

Key Knowledge Areas:

- Install, upgrade and uninstall Debian binary packages

- Find packages containing specific files or libraries which may or may not be installed

- Obtain package information like version, content, dependencies, package integrity and installation status (whether or not the package is installed)

Terms and Utilities:

/etc/apt/sources.list	apt-get
dpkg	apt-cache
dpkg-reconfigure	aptitude

102.5 Use RPM and YUM package management
Weight: 3
Description: Candidates should be able to perform package management using RPM and YUM tools.

Key Knowledge Areas:

- Install, re-install, upgrade and remove packages using RPM and YUM

- Obtain information on RPM packages such as version, status, dependencies, integrity and signatures

- Determine what files a package provides, as well as find which package a specific file comes from

Terms and Utilities:

rpm	/etc/yum.repos.d/
rpm2cpio	yum
/etc/yum.conf	yumdownloader

Topic 103: GNU and Unix Commands

103.1 Work on the command line
Weight: 4
Description: Candidates should be able to interact with shells and commands using the command line. The objective assumes the Bash shell.

Key Knowledge Areas:

- Use single shell commands and one line command sequences to perform basic tasks on the command line

- Use and modify the shell environment including defining, referencing and exporting environment variables

- Use and edit command history

- Invoke commands inside and outside the defined path

Terms and Utilities:

bash	pwd	uname
echo	set	history
env	unset	.bash_history
export	man	

103.2 Process text streams using filters

Weight: 3

Description: Candidates should be able to apply filters to text streams.

Key Knowledge Areas:

- Send text files and output streams through text utility filters to modify the output using standard UNIX commands found in the GNU textutils package

Terms and Utilities:

cat	nl	tail
cut	od	tr
expand	paste	unexpand
fmt	pr	uniq
head	sed	wc
join	sort	
less	split	

103.3 Perform basic file management

Weight: 4

Description: Candidates should be able to use the basic Linux commands to manage files and directories.

Key Knowledge Areas:

- Copy, move and remove files and directories individually

- Copy multiple files and directories recursively

- Remove files and directories recursively

- Use simple and advanced wildcard specifications in commands

- Using find to locate and act on files based on type, size, or time

- Usage of tar, cpio and dd

Terms and Utilities:

cp	rmdir	gzip
find	touch	gunzip
mkdir	tar	bzip2
mv	cpio	xz
ls	dd	file globbing
rm	file	

103.4 Use streams, pipes and redirects
Weight: 4

Description: Candidates should be able to redirect streams and connect them in order to efficiently process textual data. Tasks include redirecting standard input, standard output and standard error, piping the output of one command to the input of another command, using the output of one command as arguments to another command and sending output to both stdout and a file.

Key Knowledge Areas:

- Redirecting standard input, standard output and standard error

- Pipe the output of one command to the input of another command

- Use the output of one command as arguments to another command

- Send output to both stdout and a file

Terms and Utilities:

tee

xargs

103.5 Create, monitor and kill processes
Weight: 4

Description: Candidates should be able to perform basic process management.

Key Knowledge Areas:

- Run jobs in the foreground and background

- Signal a program to continue running after logout

- Monitor active processes

- Select and sort processes for display

- Send signals to processes

Terms and Utilities:

&	nohup	pgrep
bg	ps	pkill
fg	top	killall
jobs	free	screen
kill	uptime	

103.6 Modify process execution priorities
Weight: 2
Description: Candidates should be able to manage process execution priorities.
Key Knowledge Areas:

- Know the default priority of a job that is created

- Run a program with higher or lower priority than the default

- Change the priority of a running process

Terms and Utilities:

nice	renice
ps	top

103.7 Search text files using regular expressions
Weight: 2
Description: Candidates should be able to manipulate files and text data using regular expressions. This objective includes creating simple regular expressions containing several notational elements. It also includes using regular expression tools to perform searches through a filesystem or file content.
Key Knowledge Areas:

- Create simple regular expressions containing several notational elements

- Use regular expression tools to perform searches through a filesystem or file content

Terms and Utilities:

grep	sed
egrep	regex(7)
fgrep	

103.8 Perform basic file editing operations using vi
Weight: 3
Description: Candidates should be able to edit text files using vi. This objective includes vi navigation, basic vi modes, inserting, editing, deleting, copying and finding text.

Key Knowledge Areas:

- Navigate a document using vi

- Use basic vi modes

- Insert, edit, delete, copy and find text

Terms and Utilities:

vi	i, o, a
/, ?	c, d, p, y, dd, yy
h,j,k,l	ZZ, :w!, :q!, :e!

Topic 104: Devices, Linux Filesystems, Filesystem Hierarchy Standard

104.1 Create partitions and filesystems
Weight: 2
Description: Candidates should be able to configure disk partitions and then create filesystems on media such as hard disks. This includes the handling of swap partitions.

Key Knowledge Areas:

- Manage MBR partition tables

- Use various mkfs commands to create various filesystems such as:

- ext2/ext3/ext4

- XFS

- VFAT

- Awareness of ReiserFS and Btrfs

- Basic knowledge of gdisk and parted with GPT

Terms and Utilities:

fdisk	parted
gdisk	mkfs
mkswap	

104.2 Maintain the integrity of filesystems
Weight: 2
Description: Candidates should be able to maintain a standard filesystem, as well as the extra data associated with a journaling filesystem.

Key Knowledge Areas:

- Verify the integrity of filesystems

- Monitor free space and inodes

- Repair simple filesystem problems

Terms and Utilities:

du	mke2fs	XFS tools (such as xfs_
df	debugfs	metadump and xfs_info)
fsck	dumpe2fs	
e2fsck	tune2fs	

104.3 Control mounting and unmounting of filesystems
Weight: 3
Description: Candidates should be able to configure the mounting of a filesystem.
Key Knowledge Areas:

- Manually mount and unmount filesystems

- Configure filesystem mounting on bootup

- Configure user mountable removable filesystems

Terms and Utilities:

/etc/fstab	mount
/media/	umount

104.4 Manage disk quotas
Weight: 1
Description: Candidates should be able to manage disk quotas for users.
Key Knowledge Areas:

- Set up a disk quota for a filesystem

- Edit, check and generate user quota reports

Terms and Utilities:

quota	repquota
edquota	quotaon

104.5 Manage file permissions and ownership
Weight: 3
Description: Candidates should be able to control file access through the proper use of permissions and ownerships.
Key Knowledge Areas:

- Manage access permissions on regular and special files as well as directories
- Use access modes such as suid, sgid and the sticky bit to maintain security
- Know how to change the file creation mask
- Use the group field to grant file access to group members

Terms and Utilities:

chmod	chown
umask	chgrp

104.6 Create and change hard and symbolic links
Weight: 2
Description: Candidates should be able to create and manage hard and symbolic links to a file.
Key Knowledge Areas:

- Create links
- Identify hard and/or soft links
- Copying versus linking files
- Use links to support system administration tasks

Terms and Utilities:

ln
ls

104.7 Find system files and place files in the correct location
Weight: 2

Description: Candidates should be thoroughly familiar with the Filesystem Hierarchy Standard (FHS), including typical file locations and directory classifications.

Key Knowledge Areas:

- Understand the correct locations of files under the FHS

- Find files and commands on a Linux system

- Know the location and purpose of important file and directories as defined in the FHS

Terms and Utilities:

find	which
locate	type
updatedb	/etc/updatedb.conf
whereis	

LPIC-1 Exam 102

Exam Covered: LPIC-1 102 (102-400) also available as CompTIA Linux+ (LX0-104); Exam 2 of 2 to obtain LPIC-1 Linux Server Professional certification

Topic 105: Shells, Scripting and Data Management

105.1 Customize and use the shell environment

Weight: 4

Description: Candidates should be able to customize shell environments to meet users' needs. Candidates should be able to modify global and user profiles.

Key Knowledge Areas:

- Set environment variables (e.g., PATH) at login or when spawning a new shell

- Write Bash functions for frequently used sequences of commands

- Maintain skeleton directories for new user accounts

- Set command search path with the proper directory

The following is a partial list of the used files, terms and utilities:

.	set	~/.bash_logout
source	unset	function
/etc/bash.bashrc	~/.bash_profile	alias
/etc/profile	~/.bash_login	lists
env	~/.profile	
export	~/.bashrc	

105.2 Customize or write simple scripts
Weight: 4

Description: Candidates should be able to customize existing scripts, or write simple new Bash scripts.

Key Knowledge Areas:

- Use standard sh syntax (loops, tests)

- Use command substitution

- Test return values for success or failure or other information provided by a command

- Perform conditional mailing to the superuser

- Correctly select the script interpreter through the shebang (#!) line

- Manage the location, ownership, execution and suid-rights of scripts

Terms and Utilities:

for	while
test	seq
if	exec
read	

105.3 SQL data management
Weight: 2

Description: Candidates should be able to query databases and manipulate data using basic SQL commands. This objective includes performing queries involving joining of 2 tables and/or subselects.

Key Knowledge Areas:

- Use of basic SQL commands

- Perform basic data manipulation

Terms and Utilities:

insert	delete	group by
update	from	order by
select	where	join

Topic 106: User Interfaces and Desktops

106.1 Install and configure X11
Weight: 2
Description: Candidates should be able to install and configure X11.
Key Knowledge Areas:

- Verify that the video card and monitor are supported by an X server

- Awareness of the X font server

- Basic understanding and knowledge of the X Window configuration file

Terms and Utilities:

/etc/X11/xorg.conf	xwininfo
xhost	xdpyinfo
DISPLAY	X

106.2 Setup a display manager
Weight: 1
Description: Candidates should be able to describe the basic features and configuration of the LightDM display manager. This objective covers awareness of the display managers XDM (X Display Manger), GDM (Gnome Display Manager) and KDM (KDE Display Manager).
Key Knowledge Areas:

- Basic configuration of LightDM

- Turn the display manager on or off

- Change the display manager greeting

- Awareness of XDM, KDM and GDM

Terms and Utilities:

lightdm

/etc/lightdm/

106.3 Accessibility
Weight: 1
Description: Demonstrate knowledge and awareness of accessibility technologies.
Key Knowledge Areas:

- Basic knowledge of keyboard accessibility settings (AccessX)

- Basic knowledge of visual settings and themes

- Basic knowledge of assistive technology (ATs)

Terms and Utilities:

Sticky/Repeat Keys	Print Desktop Themes	Gestures (used at login, for example GDM)
Slow/Bounce/Toggle Keys	Screen Reader	
Mouse Keys	Braille Display	Orca
High Contrast/Large	Screen Magnifier	GOK
	On-Screen Keyboard	emacspeak

Topic 107: Administrative Tasks

107.1 Manage user and group accounts and related system files
Weight: 5
Description: Candidates should be able to add, remove, suspend and change user accounts.
Key Knowledge Areas:

- Add, modify and remove users and groups

- Manage user/group info in password/group databases

- Create and manage special purpose and limited accounts

Terms and Utilities:

/etc/passwd	getent	useradd
/etc/shadow	groupadd	userdel
/etc/group	groupdel	usermod
/etc/skel/	groupmod	
chage	passwd	

107.2 Automate system administration tasks by scheduling jobs
Weight: 4

Description: Candidates should be able to use cron or anacron to run jobs at regular intervals and to use at to run jobs at a specific time.

Key Knowledge Areas:

- Manage cron and at jobs

- Configure user access to cron and at services

- Configure anacron

Terms and Utilities:

/etc/cron.	/etc/crontab	at
{d,daily,hourly,monthly,weekly}/	/etc/cron.allow	atq
	/etc/cron.deny	atrm
/etc/at.deny	/var/spool/cron/	anacron
/etc/at.allow	crontab	/etc/anacrontab

107.3 Localisation and internationalisation
Weight: 3

Description: Candidates should be able to localize a system in a different language than English. As well, an understanding of why LANG=C is useful when scripting.

Key Knowledge Areas:

- Configure locale settings and environment variables

- Configure timezone settings and environment variables

Terms and Utilities:

/etc/timezone	LC_ALL	date
/etc/localtime	LANG	iconv
/	TZ	UTF-8
usr/share/zoneinfo	/usr/bin/locale	ISO-8859
/	tzselect	ASCII
LC_*	timedatectl	Unicode

Topic 108: Essential System Services

108.1 Maintain system time
Weight: 3

Description: Candidates should be able to properly maintain the system time and synchronize the clock via NTP.

Key Knowledge Areas:

- Set the system date and time

- Set the hardware clock to the correct time in UTC

- Configure the correct timezone

- Basic NTP configuration

- Knowledge of using the pool.ntp.org service

- Awareness of the ntpq command

Terms and Utilities:

/usr/share/zoneinfo/	
/etc/timezone	/etc/ntp.conf
/etc/localtime	date
hwclock	ntpdate
ntpd	pool.ntp.org

108.2 System logging
Weight: 3

Description: Candidates should be able to configure the syslog daemon. This objective also includes configuring the logging daemon to send log output to a central log server or accept log output as a central log server. Use of the systemd journal subsystem is covered. Also, awareness of rsyslog and syslog-ng as alternative logging systems is included.

Key Knowledge Areas:

- Configuration of the syslog daemon

- Understanding of standard facilities, priorities and actions

- Configuration of logrotate

- Awareness of rsyslog and syslog-ng

Terms and Utilities:

syslog.conf	logrotate	/
syslogd	/etc/logrotate.conf	etc/systemd/journa ld.conf
klogd	/etc/logrotate.d/	
/var/log/	journalctl	/var/log/journal/
logger		

108.3 Mail Transfer Agent (MTA) basics
Weight: 3

Description: Candidates should be aware of the commonly available MTA programs and be able to perform basic forward and alias configuration on a client host. Other configuration files are not covered.

Key Knowledge Areas:

- Create e-mail aliases

- Configure e-mail forwarding

- Knowledge of commonly available MTA programs (postfix, sendmail, qmail, exim) (no configuration)

Terms and Utilities:

~/.forward	newaliases	sendmail
sendmail	mail	exim
emulation layer	mailq	qmail
commands	postfix	

108.4 Manage printers and printing
Weight: 2

Description: Candidates should be able to manage print queues and user print jobs using CUPS and the LPD compatibility interface.

Key Knowledge Areas:

- Basic CUPS configuration (for local and remote printers)

- Manage user print queues

- Troubleshoot general printing problems

- Add and remove jobs from configured printer queues

Terms and Utilities:

CUPS configuration files, tools and utilities

/etc/cups/

lpd legacy interface (lpr, lprm, lpq)

Topic 109: Networking Fundamentals

109.1 Fundamentals of Internet protocols
Weight: 4

Description: Candidates should demonstrate a proper understanding of TCP/IP network fundamentals.

Key Knowledge Areas:

- Demonstrate an understanding of network masks and CIDR notation

- Knowledge of the differences between private and public "dotted quad" IP addresses

- Knowledge about common TCP and UDP ports and services (20, 21, 22, 23, 25, 53, 80, 110, 123, 139, 143, 161, 162, 389, 443, 465, 514, 636, 993, 995)

- Knowledge about the differences and major features of UDP, TCP and ICMP

- Knowledge of the major differences between IPv4 and IPv6

- Knowledge of the basic features of IPv6

177

Terms and Utilities:

/etc/services	Subnetting
IPv4, IPv6	TCP, UDP, ICMP

109.2 Basic network configuration
Weight: 4
Description: Candidates should be able to view, change and verify configuration settings on client hosts.

Key Knowledge Areas:

- Manually and automatically configure network interfaces

- Basic TCP/IP host configuration

- Setting a default route

Terms and Utilities:

/etc/hostname	/etc/hosts	/etc/nsswitch.conf
ifconfig	ifdown	route
ifup	ip	ping

109.3 Basic network troubleshooting
Weight: 4
Description: Candidates should be able to troubleshoot networking issues on client hosts.

Key Knowledge Areas:

- Manually and automatically configure network interfaces and routing tables to include adding, starting, stopping, restarting, deleting or reconfiguring network interfaces

- Change, view, or configure the routing table and correct an improperly set default route manually

- Debug problems associated with the network configuration

Terms and Utilities:

ifconfig	hostname	traceroute6
ip	dig	tracepath
ifup	netstat	tracepath6
ifdown	ping	netcat
route	ping6	
host	traceroute	

109.4 Configure client side DNS
Weight: 2
Description: Candidates should be able to configure DNS on a client host.
Key Knowledge Areas:

- Query remote DNS servers

- Configure local name resolution and use remote DNS servers

- Modify the order in which name resolution is done

Terms and Utilities:

/etc/hosts	host
/etc/resolv.conf	dig
/etc/nsswitch.conf	getent

Topic 110: Security

110.1 Perform security administration tasks
Weight: 3
Description: Candidates should know how to review system configuration to ensure host security in accordance with local security policies.
Key Knowledge Areas:

- Audit a system to find files with the suid/sgid bit set

- Set or change user passwords and password aging information

- Being able to use nmap and netstat to discover open ports on a system

- Set up limits on user logins, processes and memory usage

- Determine which users have logged in to the system or are currently logged in

- Basic sudo configuration and usage

Terms and Utilities:

find	chage	usermod
passwd	netstat	ulimit
fuser	sudo	who, w, last
lsof	/etc/sudoers	
nmap	su	

110.2 Setup host security
Weight: 3
Description: Candidates should know how to set up a basic level of host security.
Key Knowledge Areas:

- Awareness of shadow passwords and how they work

- Turn off network services not in use

- Understand the role of TCP wrappers

Terms and Utilities:

/etc/nologin	/etc/xinetd.conf	/etc/init.d/
/etc/passwd	/etc/inetd.d/	/etc/hosts.allow
/etc/shadow	/etc/inetd.conf	/etc/hosts.deny
/etc/xinetd.d/	/etc/inittab	

110.3 Securing data with encryption
Weight: 3
Description: The candidate should be able to use public key techniques to secure data and communication.
Key Knowledge Areas:

- Perform basic OpenSSH 2 client configuration and usage

- Understand the role of OpenSSH 2 server host keys

- Perform basic GnuPG configuration, usage and revocation

- Understand SSH port tunnels (including X11 tunnels)

Terms and Utilities:

ssh	~/.ssh/id_dsa and id_dsa.pub
ssh-keygen	/etc/ssh/ssh_host_rsa_key and
ssh-agent	ssh_host_rsa_key.pub
ssh-add	/etc/ssh/ssh_host_dsa_key and
~/.ssh/id_rsa and id_rsa.pub	ssh_host_dsa_key.pub
~/.ssh/authorized_keys ssh_known_hosts	
gpg ~/.gnupg/	

Index

A

Accessibility, 94–96
Administrative tasks
    arguments, 101
    attributes, 101
    Linux distributions, 100
    Linux filesystem, 99
    passwd, 100
    password vault software packages, 101
    useradd, 100
    users, 99–102
Anacron, 104–105
Aptitude package manager, 26
'at' program command, 105
Attributes, 101
Autogenerated symlink, 137
Automate system administration, 174

B

Bash shell, 31–33
Basic file management, 164–165
Boot manager, installation and
    configuration, 21

C

Calibre's private repository, 28
Classless Inter-Domain
    Routing (CIDR), 126
Client side DNS, 136–138, 179
Coldplug, 159
Common Unix Printing System (CUPS), 120
CompTIA Linux+, 159
Control mounting, 168
cpio archive tool, 40
cron system, 103–104, 116

D

Data Management, 170–172
Debian package management system,
    119, 141, 162–163
Desktops, 172–173
Device management
    administrators and developers, 12
    browser-based web
        conferencing tool, 13
    circuit boards, 12
    Internet searches, 13
    Linux kernel modules, 11–12
    troubleshooting, 12
    USB drives and cameras, 11
/dev/null directory, 147
Disk partitioning
    default, 17
    GUI GParted tool, 19–20
    Logical Volume Manager
        (LVM), 20–21
    performance and security, 17
    swap file, 17
    Ubuntu server installation
        process, 18–19
Disk quotas, 61–62, 168
Display manager
    autologin feature, 91
    commands, 92
    Gnome-Fallback, 91
    LightDM login screen, 90, 92
    login screen, 90
    optional entries, 91
    pull-down menu, 91, 93
    router, 93
    settings, 91
    X11 protocol, 90
    xhost, 93

© David Clinton 2016
D. Clinton, *Practical LPIC-1 Linux Certification Study Guide*,
DOI 10.1007/978-1-4842-2358-1

Domain Name System (DNS), 136–138
DOS.BAT files, 106
Dwell Click, 96
Dynamic Host Configuration Protocol
(DHCP), 133

■ E

Editing operations, 167
Encryption
algorithm, 149
e-mail attachments, 148
wireless/public digital networks, 148
English-speaking countries, 107
Essential system services, 175
/etc/pam.d/system-auth file, 141
/etc/resolv.conf file, 137
/etc/rsyslog.d/ directory, 115
/etc/security/limits.conf file, 145
/etc/shadow file, 99
/etc/ssh/sshd_config file, 150
/etc/sudoers file, 142
/etc/systemd/, 161
/etc/xinetd.conf configuration file, 146
/etc/xinetd.d/, 147
Execution priorities, 45–46

■ F

Fedora installation, 9
FHS. See Filesystem Hierarchy Standard
(FHS)
Figaro, 101
File archives, 40
File management, 37–39
File permissions, 169
Filesystem Hierarchy Standard (FHS),
68–69, 167–168, 170
ForwardX11 line, 152
Fully qualified domain names
(FQDNs), 137

■ G

gedit, 152
Gnome Onscreen Keyboard (GOK), 95
Gnu and Unix commands
Bash shell, 31–33
description, 31
execution priorities, 45–46
file archives, 40

file management, 37–39
Regular Expression (REGEX), 46–47
streams, pipes and redirects, 41–42
text stream processing, 33–37
vi editor, 48–49
GnuPG Config, 152–155
Gnu Privacy Guard (GPG), 152
gpg --export, 154
gpg --import, 154
GRand Unified Bootloader (GRUB)
advanced menu, 4
older versions, 2–3
parameters, 4–5
version 2 boot menu, 3
Graphic functionality, 152
Graphic user interface (GUI), 87
grep, 136
Groups
directory, 102
/etc/group file, 103
sensitive documents, 102
usermod-G, 102
GRUB. See GRand Unified Bootloader
(GRUB)
guid (group) permissions, 145
GUID Partition Table (GPT), 54–55

■ H

Hard and symbolic links, 169
Hardware clock, 111–112
Hardware settings, 159
hctosys, 112
Host security
built-in security benefits, 146
hosts.deny, 148
nonroot log, 146
run-level control system, 146
TCP wrappers, 147
UDP versions, 147
vsftpd file, 147
xinetd file configuration, 147, 148
Hotplug, 159

■ I, J

includedir /etc/xinetd.d line, 147
Inetd, 146
InputDevice, 89
Integrity of filesystems, 168
Internationalization, 106–109, 174–175

Internet Message Access
        Protocol (IMAP), 118
Internet protocols, 177–178
IPv4 address, 126–127
IPv6 protocol, 128–129

■ K

KDE Display Manager, 172
KeePassX, 101
Kernel-level driver, 134

■ L

LightDM manager, 90, 91
Linux boot process
    BIOS, 1
    cloud platform, 1
    GRUB advanced menu, 4
    GRUB stage, 2–5
    hardware environment, 1
    pseudo filesystems, 10–11
    run levels, 7–9
    steps, 2
    temporary filesystem (tmpfs), 2
    testing, 13–15
    troubleshooting, 5–6
Linux Filesystems, 167–168
Linux installation, 161–162
Linux Locale Values, 108
Linux OS, 99
LiSt Open Files (lsof), 143
Localization, 106–109, 174–175
logger, 116
logrotate, 117–118
lp daemon, 121
lpd command-line interface, 121
LPIC-1 exam
    CompTIA Linux+, 170
    professional certification, 159
lsof tools, 144

■ M

Mail Transfer Agent (MTA)
        basics, 118–120, 176

■ N

nameservers, 137
netcat, 136

Network Address Translation (NAT), 127–128
    address ranges, 127
    attached devices, 127
    IPv4 network, 128
    IPv6 protocol, 128–129
    network translation, 127
Network configuration, 178
    command line, 132
    Debian/Ubuntu machines, 132
    DHCP NAT address, 131
    gateway device, 133
    ifconfig, 131
    interface, 131
    LPIC exam, 131
Network interface card (NIC), 13
Network time protocol (NTP), 112–114
Network troubleshooting
    DHCP server, 134
    external interface, 134
    Internet provider, 135
    IPv6, 135
    kernel modules, 134
    Linux, 133
    netstat, 136
    ping, 135
    rebooting, 135
    router address, 135
ntpdate program, 112
ntpq shell, 113

■ O

OpenSSH 2 server, 180
OpenSSH server package, 149–150
Ownership, 169

■ P, Q

Package management, 161–162
Package managers
    APT system, 23–26
    download and install, software, 23
    dpkg, 23–24
    RPM, 27
    system libraries, 23
    yum, 27
Partitions and filesystems
    Boot field, 54
    btrfs, 55
    control mounting and
        unmounting, 59–60
    disk quotas, 61–62

Partitions and filesystems (*cont.*)
    ext2, 55
    ext3 and ext4, 55
    FHS, 68–69
    file permissions and ownership
        letters, 62–63
        numbers, 64
        subjects, 63
        suid, sgid and sticky bit, 65–66
        umask, 64–65
    GUID Partition Table (GPT), 54–55
    hard and symbolic links, 66–67
    Master Boot Record (MBR), 53
    monitoring, 56
    preventive maintenance, 57
    reiserfs, 55
    repair, 57–58
    search tools, 69–70
    swap files, 55
    VFAT, 55
    XFS, 55
Passwordless access, 150–151
Password-protected screensaver, 142
Personal Package Archive (PPA), 28
Pluggable Authentication
        Module (PAM), 141
Post Office Protocol 3 (POP3), 118
Printers, 120–121, 177
Printing, 120–121, 177
Process execution priorities, 166
Process management
    background, 43–45
    killing, 45
    monitoring, 42–43
Pseudo filesystems, 10–11

■ **R**

Real-time clock (RTC), 111
Red Hat Enterprise Linux, 27
Regular Expression (REGEX), 46–47
Remote backups, 99
RFC 863 discard server, 147
rsyslog, 114
Runlevels/boot targets, 161

■ **S**

Scripting, 170–172
Search text files, 166
Secure Shell network connectivity tool, 9

Securing data, 180
    LPI, 141
    national foreign service, 141
Security administration tasks, 179–180
Service ports, 129–130
Setup host security, 180
Shared libraries, 21–22
Shells, 170–172
    alias command, 74
    ~/.bash_logout controls, 74
    configuration files, 74
    functions, 74
    login and non-login, 73–74
Shell scripts
    alias and function, 75
    commands, 75
    inputs, 76–77
    loops, 78–80
    shebang, 75
    structure, 75
    testing values, 77–78
Simple Mail Transfer Protocol (SMTP), 118
SQL data management
    elements, 81
    fields, 83
    MySQL, 80–81
    online company, 80
    PHP, 82
    records, 84
    shippers and orders, 84
ssh-agent, 151
ssh_host_dsa, 150
statsdir setting, 114
Streams, 165
Super-turbocharged graphics, 96
Synaptic package manager, 25
syslogd, 114–116
Systemarchitecture. *See* Linux boot
        process
System booting, 160–161
systemctl, 161
Systemd boot target, 160, 161
Systemd functionality, 107
System logging, 176
System security
    administrative users, 142
    admin shell, 142
    categories, 145
    directory hierarchy, 143
    internet-based addresses, 144
    lowercase, 141

lsof tools, 144
ownerless files, 145
password complexity, 141
password-protected
        screensaver, 142
password required, 141
ps processes, 146
sgid bit set, 145
ssh session, 143
sudo group, 142
user log ins, 142
vulnerabilities, 145
SysVinit runlevel, 160

■ **T**

Text stream processing, 33–37
Text streams, 164
Tracepath, 136
Traceroute, 136
Transmission Control
        Protocol (TCP), 125
Troubleshooting, 5–6

■ **U**

Ubuntu systems, 114
Unix Commands, 163

User Datagram Protocol
        (UDP), 125
User interfaces, 172–173
        accessibility, 94–96
        cutting-edge hardware, 87
/usr/bin/passwd binary, 145
UTF-8 encoding, 108

■ **V, W**

/var/spool/cron directory, 106

■ **X**

X11 protocol
        ATI adapters, 89
        built-in system manuals, 89
        configuration file, 87, 89
        hardware profile, 89
        server, 87
X engine, 87
X Font server, 90
xhost, 93
xorg.conf file, 88–89

■ **Y, Z**

YUM package management, 163

Get the eBook for only $4.99!

Why limit yourself?

Now you can take the weightless companion with you wherever you go and access your content on your PC, phone, tablet, or reader.

Since you've purchased this print book, we are happy to offer you the eBook for just $4.99.

Convenient and fully searchable, the PDF version enables you to easily find and copy code—or perform examples by quickly toggling between instructions and applications.

To learn more, go to http://www.apress.com/us/shop/companion or contact support@apress.com.

Printed in the United States
By Bookmasters